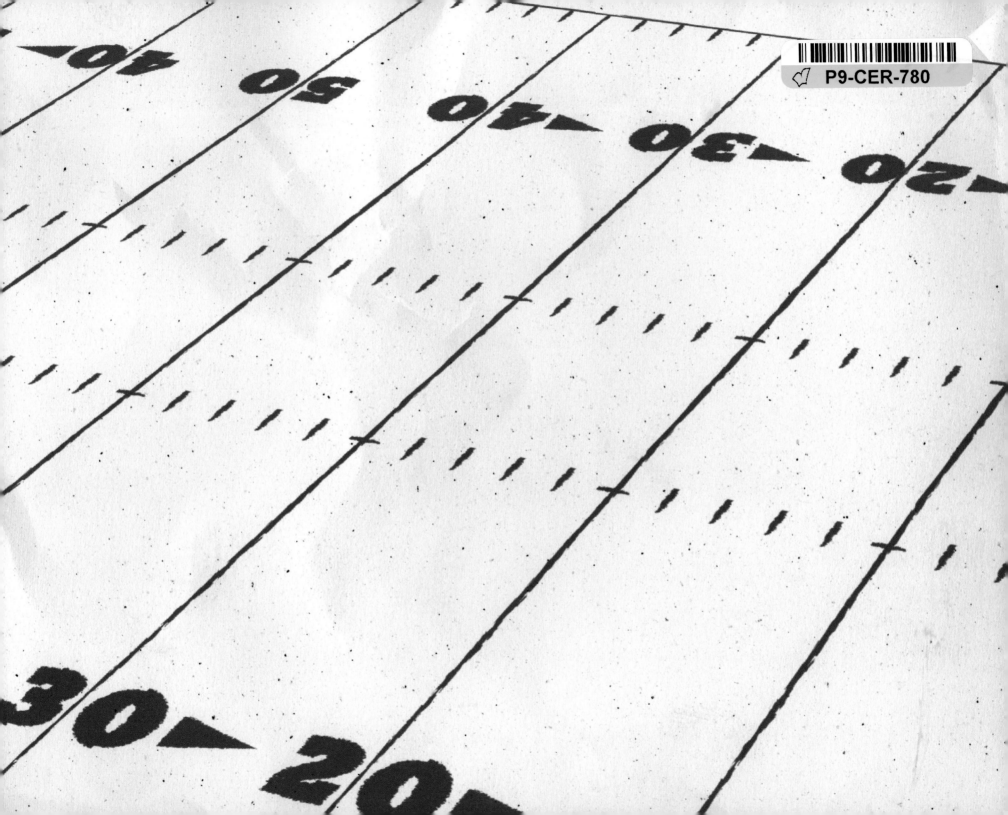

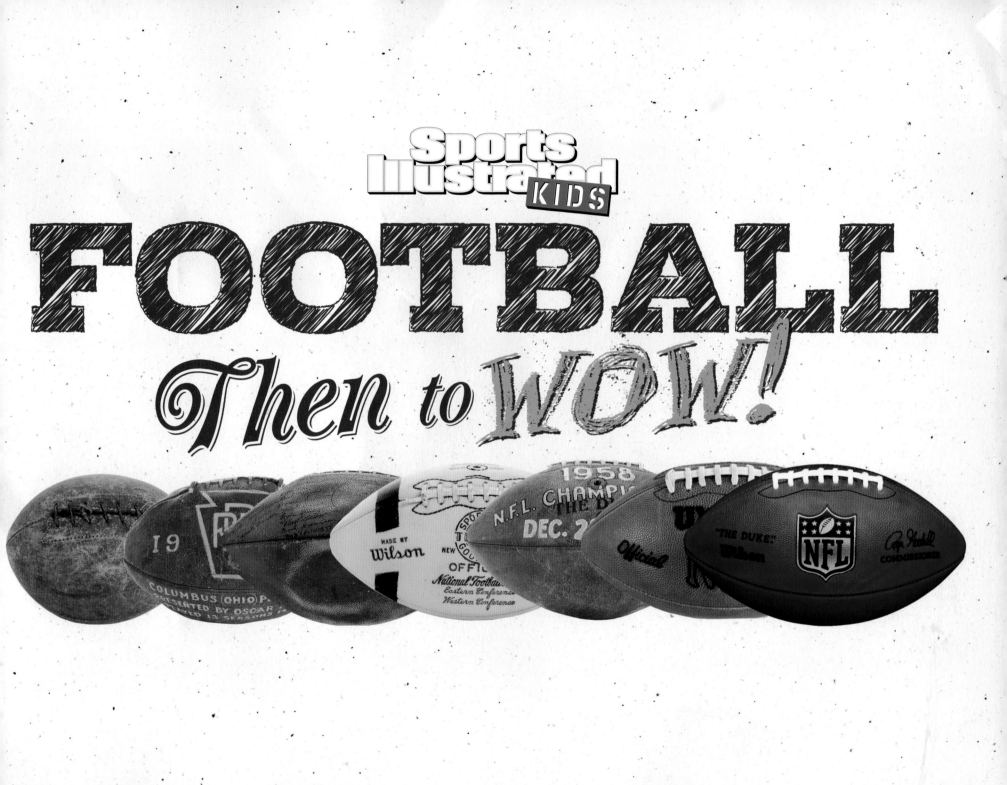

Sports Illustrated KIDS

FOOTBALL

Then to WOW!

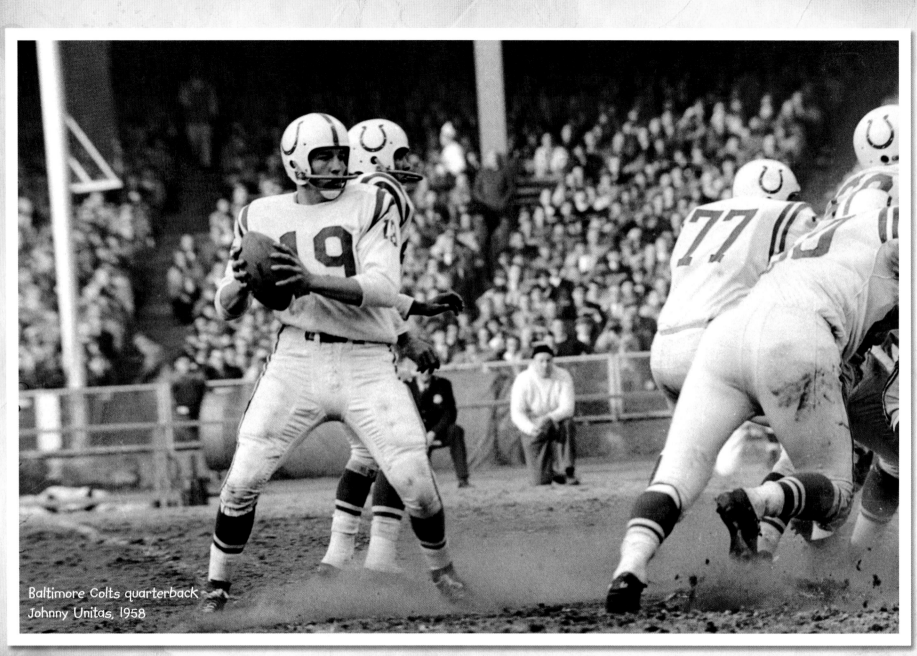

Baltimore Colts quarterback
Johnny Unitas, 1958

THEN

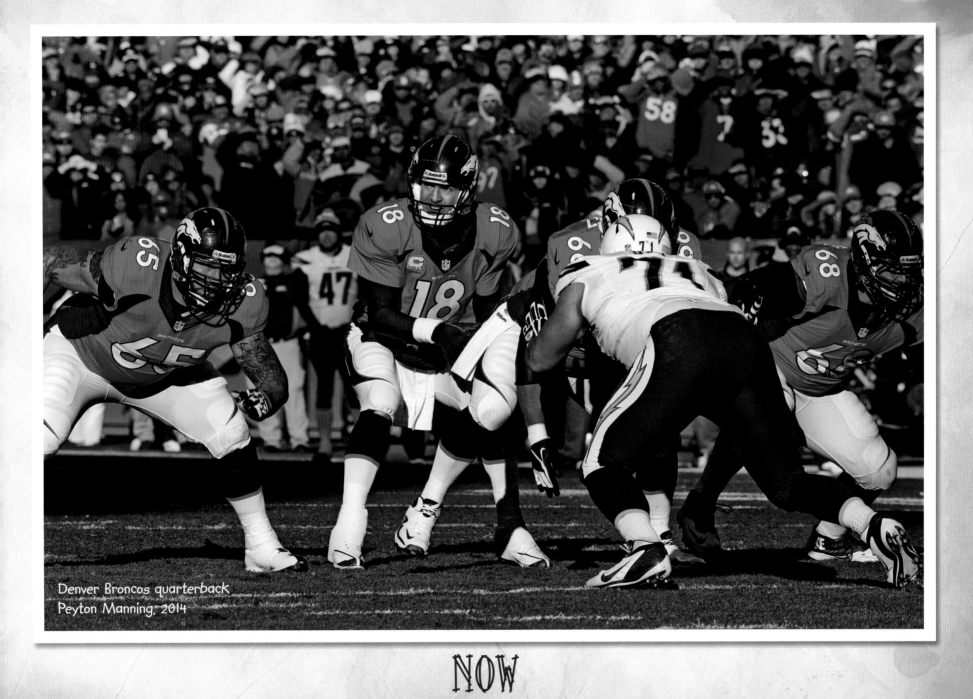

Denver Broncos quarterback
Peyton Manning, 2014

NOW

Managing Editor, SPORTS ILLUSTRATED KIDS **Bob Der**

Creative Director **Beth Bugler**

Project Editor **Andrea Woo**

Writer **Sachin Shenolikar**

Photo Editor **Annmarie Avila**

Copy Editor **Megan Collins**

Reporter **Gary Gramling**

Premedia **Geoffrey Michaud, Dan Larkin,
Gerry Burke, Brian Mai, Neal Clayton, Marco Lau**

Illustrations by **Andrew Roberts**

Copyright © 2014 Time Inc. Books

Published by Liberty Street, an imprint of Time Inc. Books
225 Liberty Street
New York, NY 10281

LIBERTY STREET and SPORTS ILLUSTRATED KIDS are trademarks of Time Inc.

ISBN: 978-1-61893-116-0
Library of Congress Control Number: 2014934080

First edition, 2014

4 TLF 17

5 7 9 8 6 4

We welcome your comments and suggestions about Time Inc. Books. Please write to us at:
Time Inc. Books
Attention: Book Editors
P.O. Box 62310
Tampa, FL 33662-2310
(800) 765-6400

timeincbooks.com

Time Inc. Books products may be purchased for business or promotional use. For information on bulk purchases, please contact Christi Crowley in the Special Sales Department at (845) 895-9858.

The CONTENTS

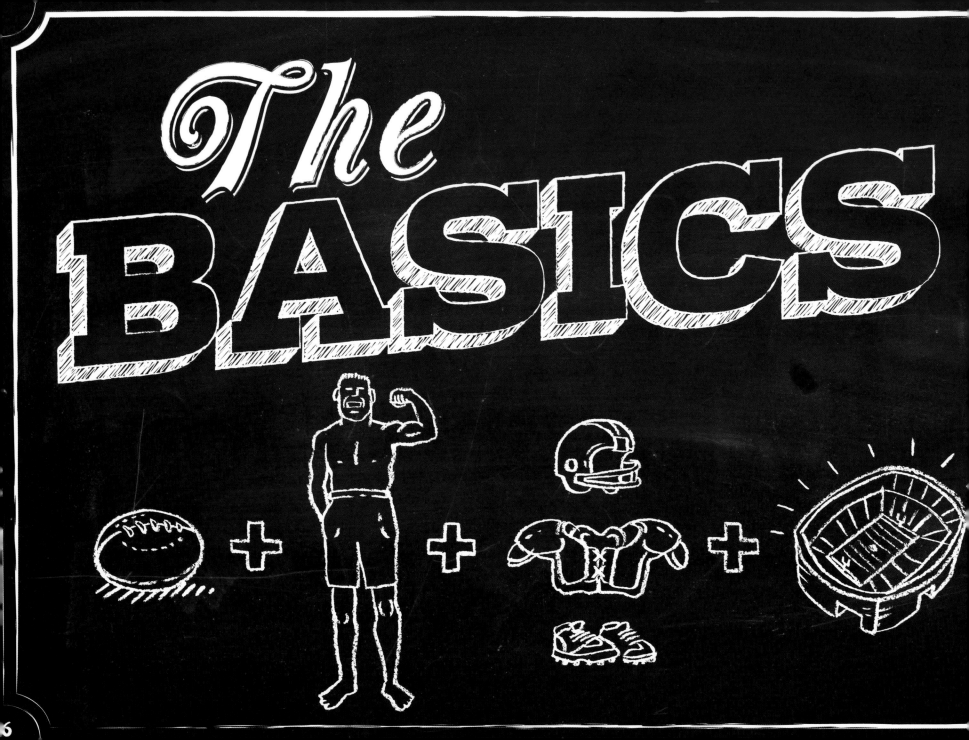

The sport of football has come a long way since it was born in 1869. Back in those days, players didn't wear pads, and passing or even carrying the ball weren't allowed! Of course, things have changed quite a bit over the years, including the equipment, the stats, the rules, and the venues where the games are played. Turn the page to see how the basic elements of the game have evolved into what we see in modern times.

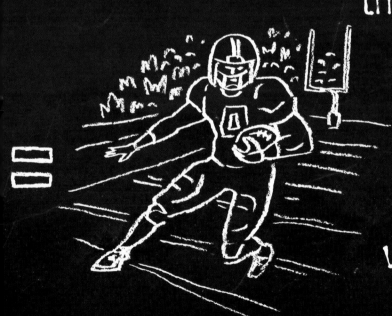

The Rules

A brief timeline of how the game has been played

There's one thing that's obvious about the game of football: It has a *lot* of rules. It has been that way ever since it was adopted from the British sport of rugby in the late 1800s. But football has also gone through a lot of change on its way to becoming the game we know and love today. Once upon a time, a touchdown was worth four points, field goals counted for five points, and helmets weren't mandatory! Here's a timeline of when the most important NFL rules were put into place over the years.

4 ~~points~~
~~5 points~~
6!

1904

A field goal went from being five points to four. In 1909, it was changed to three points.

1898

Scoring a touchdown was changed from four points to five.

1876

The first rules of football were written at the Massasoit Convention in Massachusetts, led by Yale University player and coach Walter Camp. Camp is known as the father of American football.

1906

The forward pass was made legal, but the passer had to be five yards behind the line of scrimmage when releasing the ball.

1912

A touchdown score was now worth six points.

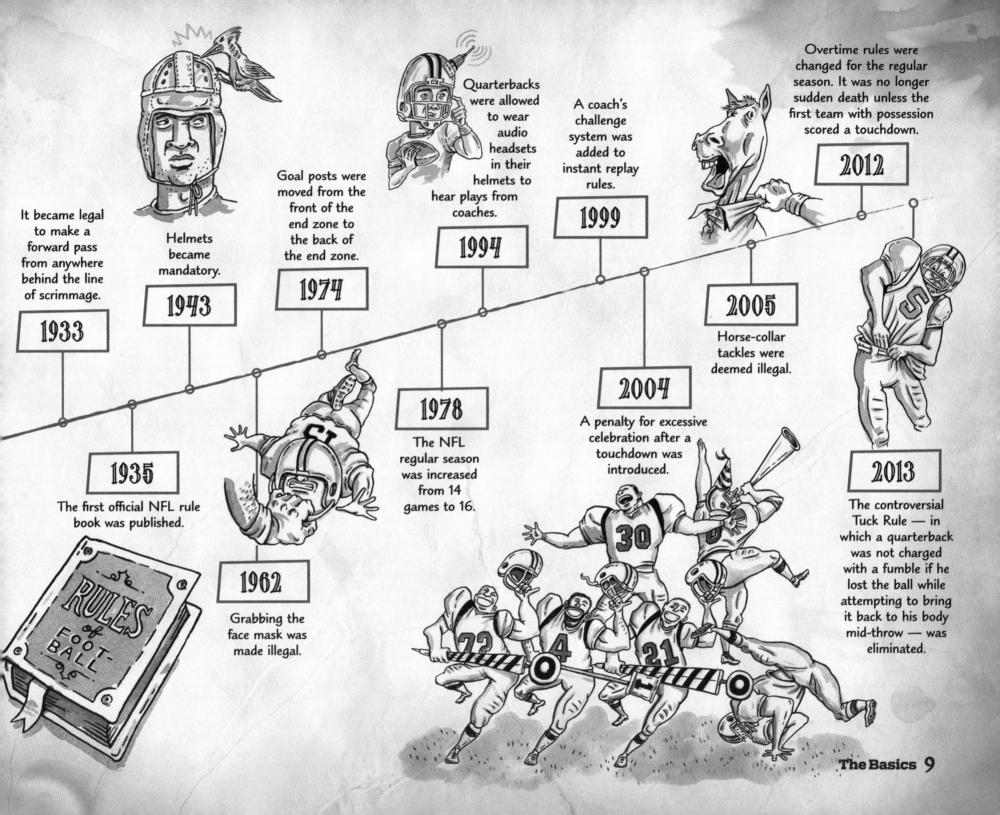

It became legal to make a forward pass from anywhere behind the line of scrimmage.

1933

1935

The first official NFL rule book was published.

Helmets became mandatory.

1943

Goal posts were moved from the front of the end zone to the back of the end zone.

1974

1962

Grabbing the face mask was made illegal.

Quarterbacks were allowed to wear audio headsets in their helmets to hear plays from coaches.

1994

1978

The NFL regular season was increased from 14 games to 16.

A coach's challenge system was added to instant replay rules.

1999

2004

A penalty for excessive celebration after a touchdown was introduced.

Overtime rules were changed for the regular season. It was no longer sudden death unless the first team with possession scored a touchdown.

2012

2005

Horse-collar tackles were deemed illegal.

2013

The controversial Tuck Rule — in which a quarterback was not charged with a fumble if he lost the ball while attempting to bring it back to his body mid-throw — was eliminated.

⇥ Late 1800s ⇤

Since football evolved from the game of rugby, the first footballs were similar to those used in that sport. A common tale is that footballs were originally made from pigs' bladders, but that is not true. They've always been made of leather. The term *pigskin* likely came from rugby players in the 1850s who created a ball out of an animal bladder wrapped in leather. It had a rough texture, like a pig's skin.

⇥ Early 1900s ⇤

The forward pass was legalized in 1906, and the ball was designed to be longer, which made it easier to grip and throw downfield. However, there was a big risk to passing: An incompletion was a turnover. Running the ball was still the most popular strategy for teams.

⇥ 1930s to '40s ⇤

By 1912, incomplete passes were no longer turnovers and more teams began incorporating passing into their game plans. By the 1930s, football design evolved to the longer shape we see today. In 1941, Wilson Sporting Goods became the official producer of NFL footballs.

⇥ Early 1950s ⇤

These white footballs were supposed to help players see passes coming their way during night games. But the light color didn't work that well. In 1956, the NFL changed to brown footballs with white end stripes for night competition.

The Ball

How the look has changed, from the shape to the color to the inscriptions

⇥ 1970s ⇤

In 1970, the Wilson ball was redesigned. THE DUKE was removed and the ball had no official name.

⇥ 2010s ⇤

After Wellington Mara died in 2005, the NFL put THE DUKE back on footballs in honor of the beloved owner. Today's footballs also have the signature of NFL commissioner Roger Goodell, along with the league's official logo.

⇥ Late 1950s to '60s ⇤

From 1941 through '69, NFL footballs were inscribed with THE DUKE in honor of New York Giants owner Wellington (Duke) Mara. His father had helped to select Wilson Sporting Goods as the NFL's official football maker.

Wellington Mara

⇥ 2000s ⇤

Every NFL ball since 1955 has been made in the Wilson factory in the small town of Ada, Ohio. The factory has 120 workers and produces 700,000 footballs a year. Modern footballs weigh 14 to 15 ounces. Their exterior is made from cowhide, and every ball has 16 lace holes.

Shoulder Pads

1890s

Early 1920s

1920s to '30s

1940s

Football players didn't wear pads in the early days of football. Instead, they put on a heavy canvas vest and jacket to absorb some of the shock from hits.

By 1920, leather shoulder pads were developed. The main purpose was to protect players' collarbones and sternums. Later, larger shoulder pads were made to protect players' ribs as well.

Equipment makers started incorporating hard plastic into shoulder pads and designing them so they extended higher above the shoulders, providing extra protection.

Tracing the evolution of body protection from flimsy jackets to the high-tech armor of today

1960s

1980s

2010s

By the 1960s, shoulder pads started becoming more body-fitting and were made of hard plastic with foam cushioning. By the '80s the plastic shell covered the players' entire chest area.

Modern shoulder pads are designed to be lightweight so they provide top-notch protection without slowing athletes down. Some pads also have built-in skin-cooling systems that activate when a player's body reaches a high temperature.

⇆ 1900s ⇆

The helmet was invented in 1896. The early ones were made of leather and their main purpose was to protect athletes' ears. The problem: Players had trouble hearing during games!

⇆ 1910s ⇆

The development of the dog-ear soft leather helmet provided more padding to the crown, better protection around the ears — and it had ear holes.

⇆ 1930s ⇆

Hard leather helmets were the main noggin protectors from the 1920s through the mid-1940s. Teams kept a simple look — the helmets had no logos, team colors, or mascot caricatures on them.

⇆ 1940s ⇆

In 1943, the NFL made a rule stating that all players had to wear helmets. In 1948, the Los Angeles Rams became the first NFL team to have a logo on its helmet. It was the idea of halfback Fred Gehrke, who got permission from the team and painted all 75 Rams helmets for that season.

Helmets

⊭ 1950s ⊭

Plastic helmets became common in the NFL in 1949. Padding was added inside for more protection, as was a single face bar. Both were major developments as helmets started taking on the characteristics of modern headgear.

⊭ 1960s & '70s ⊭

By the mid-1960s, every NFL player wore a face mask. By the '70s, air was pumped into helmet cushioning to soften the blow of hits, face masks became larger, and chin straps were added to better keep the helmet in place.

⊭ 1980s & '90s ⊭

In the mid-1980s, polycarbonate plastic helmets were introduced — these were stronger and lighter than ever before. In the '90s, radio earpieces were installed so quarterbacks could hear play calls from coaches on the sideline.

⊭ 2000s & '10s ⊭

Modern-day helmets provide full coverage of players' heads. They also have holes in the top to allow air inside and extra padding on the lining to protect the jaw and crown. Scientists are continuing to develop helmets with the hope of reducing concussions.

The development of NFL headgear, from simple leather ear protectors to colorful polycarbonate wonders of science

Stadiums

The homes of the NFL teams have grown to become larger than life

⇒ THEN ⇒

The first NFL playoff game was played in Chicago Stadium in 1932. The indoor arena held 11,000 fans and cost about $10 million to build. It was mainly used as the home of the Chicago Blackhawks hockey team.

⇔ NOW ⇔

AT&T Stadium, home of the Dallas Cowboys, is a great example of a modern football environment. It has a retractable roof, high-end restaurants, one of the world's largest high-definition TV screens, and even an art gallery. The stadium can seat more than 100,000 fans and cost more than $1 billion to build.

The Modern-Day Stadium

For the perfect example of how far football facilities have come over the past century, look no further than University of Phoenix Stadium, home of the Arizona Cardinals. The Cards' stadium was built using a mix of modern technology, artistic creativity, and a plan for preserving the environment through recycling and energy conservation. Here are some of its coolest features.

18 Miles
Approximate length of the stadium's 63,400 seats if they were placed in a straight line

$455 Million
Estimated cost to build the stadium

1.7 Million Square Feet
The stadium's size

Retractable Roof

Retractable roofs are a recent addition to football stadiums. They are crucial in places such as Phoenix, where high temperatures can make playing sports dangerous. The University of Phoenix Stadium roof allows sunlight to come through when its panels are closed, so games always have an outdoor feel. It takes about 15 minutes for the roof to open or close.

Work of Art

The Cardinals' stadium was designed to look like a barrel cactus (a common plant in Arizona) from the outside. The stadium exterior also has slim, vertical windows so fans can look at the desert horizon before heading to their seats.

Rolling Field

Arizona's movable grass field is the first of its kind in the United States. The field is placed in an 18.9-million-pound tray that is kept outside of the stadium so the grass can grow in its natural environment. The tray has an irrigation system that keeps the grass healthy. On the day of a game, the field is rolled into the stadium using steel wheel assemblies.

Going Green

Like many modern playing arenas, University of Phoenix Stadium has green initiatives that make the game-day experience more friendly to the environment. There is a strong emphasis on recycling, and motion-sensor lights and water faucets have been installed to save water and energy.

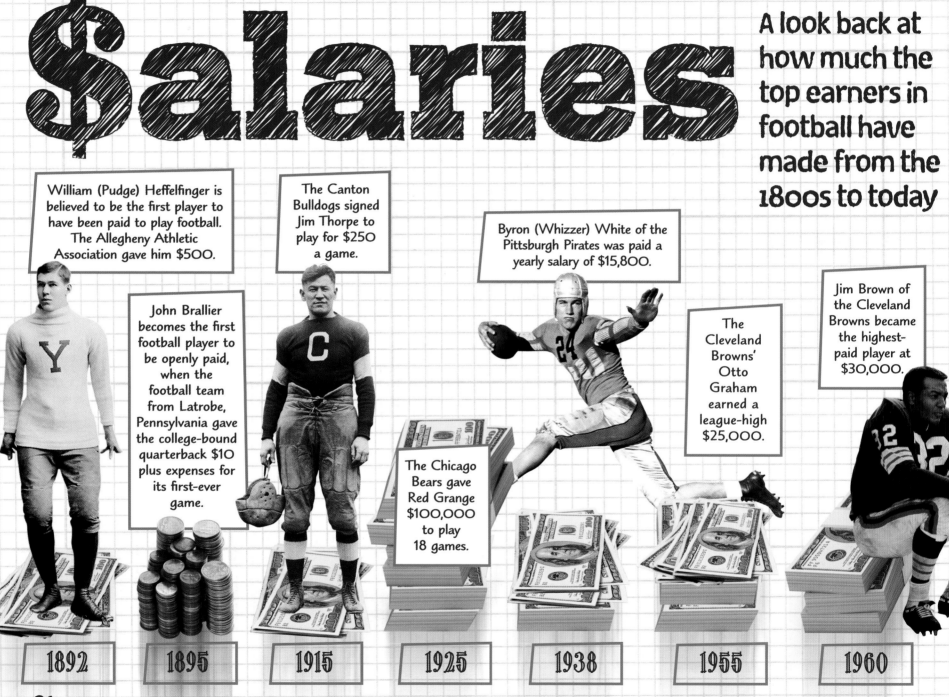

$alaries

A look back at how much the top earners in football have made from the 1800s to today

William (Pudge) Heffelfinger is believed to be the first player to have been paid to play football. The Allegheny Athletic Association gave him $500.

The Canton Bulldogs signed Jim Thorpe to play for $250 a game.

Byron (Whizzer) White of the Pittsburgh Pirates was paid a yearly salary of $15,800.

Jim Brown of the Cleveland Browns became the highest-paid player at $30,000.

John Brallier becomes the first football player to be openly paid, when the football team from Latrobe, Pennsylvania gave the college-bound quarterback $10 plus expenses for its first-ever game.

The Cleveland Browns' Otto Graham earned a league-high $25,000.

The Chicago Bears gave Red Grange $100,000 to play 18 games.

1892 1895 1915 1925 1938 1955 1960

Joe Namath was the highest-paid QB, making $500,000.

Thirteen NFL players had base salaries of at least $1 million a season. Miami Dolphins QB Dan Marino was the league's top earner at $1.45 million.

Deion Sanders of the Dallas Cowboys became the highest-paid defensive player, with a seven-year, $35 million contract.

QB Brett Favre of the Green Bay Packers earned the most ($47 million over seven years).

Dwight Freeney of the Colts became the best-paid defensive player in NFL history ($70 million over six years).

Quarterback Aaron Rodgers of the Green Bay Packers earned the most ($22 million, as part of five-year, $110-million contract).

1965

1988

1995

1997

2007

2013

The numbers that help grade player performance have grown more complex

Stats

P art of the fun of being a fan is comparing players and debating who is the best (or worst) at their position. Stats can help you back up your argument, but sometimes it's not enough to know who passed for the most yards, who scored the most touchdowns, or who had the most sacks. After all, there are many other ways to impact the game. Here are some statistics that have evolved over the years, changing the way we rate players.

Passer Rating

Since 1973 the NFL has been using a formula that calculates a QB's effectiveness, using his percentage of completions, touchdown passes, and interceptions, as well as average yards gained per attempt. **AARON RODGERS** of the Green Bay Packers is the NFL's all-time career leader in passer rating (104.9).

Yards After Contact

How do you determine the power and tenacity of a running back? By measuring the number of yards he gains after first getting hit by a defender. It's no surprise that **ADRIAN PETERSON** of the Minnesota Vikings is usually among the league leaders in this category.

Pancake Blocks

Offensive linemen don't have any official stats. However, the website Pro Football Focus devised a formula to grade offensive linemen based on how they individually perform on a play. In 2013, it ranked **JOE THOMAS**, who started 16 games for the Cleveland Browns, as the NFL's best pass protector. There is also an unofficial stat called pancake blocks — when an OL blocks a defender to the ground — that shows a lineman's dominance.

Targets

A player gets credit for a target when the QB attempts a pass to him. This stat shows how involved a player is in his team's game plan, even if he doesn't have many receptions or yards. **CALVIN JOHNSON** of the Detroit Lions was the most targeted receiver in the NFL from 2011 through '13.

Quarterback Hurries

The job of a defensive end like Pro Bowler **J.J. WATT** of the Houston Texans is to put pressure on opposing QBs. Sometimes he'll take the quarterback down for a sack, but there are other times when he'll get close, forcing the signal-caller to rush his throw. These stats, called quarterback hurries, are not official.

Passes Defensed

A player is credited with a pass defensed when he breaks up or intercepts a pass. Cornerback **DARRELLE REVIS** set the NFL single-season record for passes defensed in 2009, when he had 31 for the New York Jets.

Football has come a long way thanks to the stars on the field and the unique talents they have brought to the game over the years. Players are constantly displaying new styles and skills, building on the breakthroughs and accomplishments of the guys before them. Turn the page to read about the stars who shaped the way positions and records have transformed into what we see today.

Quarterbacks

Signal-callers have always been the biggest stars and the most revolutionary players in the game

= 1930s & '40s =
Sammy Baugh

Even though the forward pass was legalized in the early 1900s, football largely remained a run-based game. That is, until Slingin' Sammy Baugh joined the Washington Redskins in 1937. With his strong, accurate right arm, Baugh showed that it was possible to move the ball downfield through the air. In 16 seasons with Washington, Baugh won six passing titles and helped establish the style of offense that we see today. Baugh was the perfect athlete for a time when football players often played offense, defense, and special teams. In 1943, he led the NFL in passes completed as a QB, interceptions as a defensive back, and punting yards!

= 1940s & '50s =
Otto Graham

As Baugh entered his prime in the 1940s, another future Hall of Famer, Graham, was getting his start. There will never be a winner like Automatic Otto, who led the Cleveland Browns to the championship game in each of his 10 pro seasons. He won four AAFC (All-American Football Conference) and three NFL titles. Graham was a stellar all-around athlete who made plays with his arm and legs. He and head coach Paul Brown revolutionized the sport with their modernized passing game, using precision timing routes to outmaneuver defenses. He was also the first player to wear a face mask on his helmet.

⊨ 1950s & '60s ⊨
Johnny Unitas

A major development in the game of football was the emergence of the AFL (American Football League), a new league that rivaled the NFL in the 1960s. Quarterbacks in the AFL — such as Joe Namath of the New York Jets, who was the first QB to throw for 4,000 yards in a season — played a pass-oriented style. NFL teams stuck with more conservative run-based attacks, with one big exception: The NFL's Baltimore Colts had a superstar signal-caller in Johnny Unitas. From 1956 to '60, Johnny U. threw a touchdown pass in 47 straight games, a record that stood for nearly 52 years until Drew Brees of the New Orleans Saints broke it in 2012.

The Jets' Joe Namath was the first QB to throw for 4,000 yards in a season.

⊨ 1970s ⊨
Terry Bradshaw

The AFL and NFL merged in 1970, and the NFL took on the pass-focused qualities of its onetime rival. In 1974, the NFL passed a series of rules that limited defensive contact on receivers downfield. This played to the strength of strong-armed quarterbacks such as Terry Bradshaw, who led the Pittsburgh Steelers to four Super Bowl wins during the decade. In 1971, the New Orleans Saints chose Archie Manning with the Number 2 pick in the draft. Manning could make plays through the air and on the ground, but he didn't have a strong enough supporting cast to become a star in the pros. Of course, Archie's experience did factor into the later success of his sons, future star QBs Peyton and Eli.

Quarterbacks

⊰ 1980s ⊱
Joe Montana

This decade spawned two vastly different styles. Joe Montana led the San Francisco 49ers to four Super Bowl titles with a West Coast offense that dominated games with short, accurate passing. In the AFC, Dan Marino used the deep ball to lead an explosive Miami Dolphins offense. He tossed an NFL-record 48 touchdown passes in 1984.

The Dolphins' Dan Marino was a true gunslinger with the deep ball.

Montana replaced by Steve Young

⊰ 1990s ⊱
John Elway

In the mid '90s, the NFL tweaked its rules, further restricting the contact that defensive backs could make on receivers. As the rules continued to favor downfield passing, strong-armed QBs like John Elway of the Denver Broncos thrived. Elway won back-to-back Super Bowl titles with the Broncos, during the 1997 and '98 seasons. Meanwhile, Steve Young, who had taken over as quarterback for the 49ers, added a new dimension to the West Coast offense, making plays with his legs as well as his strong left arm. In St. Louis, Rams QB Kurt Warner engineered a high-powered, record-breaking offense nicknamed the Greatest Show on Turf.

⊨ 2000s ⊨
Peyton Manning

As technology improved and studying game film became an art form, Peyton Manning took quarterbacking to another level with his unparalleled work ethic and preparation. Knowing the ins and outs of opposing defenses allowed Manning to make adjustments to plays at the line of scrimmage. At the same time, Michael Vick, one of the greatest pure athletes ever to put on a uniform, redefined what it meant to be a running quarterback. As the rules of the game continued to allow receivers to move freely without downfield contact from defenders, QB's passing numbers reached new heights. In 2007, Tom Brady of the New England Patriots set an NFL single-season record with 50 touchdown passes.

With his explosive athleticism, Michael Vick took dual-threat quarterbacking to a whole new level.

Tom Brady established a new passing mark with 50 touchdown passes in 2007.

⊨ 2010s ⊨
Russell Wilson

A new group of young signal-callers are making a big impact on the game, led by Russell Wilson of the Seattle Seahawks, Andrew Luck of the Indianapolis Colts, and Colin Kaepernick of the 49ers. All three combine the qualities of the legendary quarterbacks who came before them — blending great smarts, strong, accurate throwing, and the ability to run. Wilson proved that this new breed of quarterback could produce results: He led the Seahawks to a win in Super Bowl XLVIII.

Peyton Manning's smarts

+

John Elway's arm

+

Otto Graham's legs

Running

Two rushing greats go head-to-head

THEN

Jim Brown

1957–65	**CAREER**
6'2", 232 pounds	**HEIGHT, WEIGHT**
Defenders did not have an easy time tackling Brown, a bruising back with an awesome combination of power and speed.	**STYLE**
Brown led the NFL in rushing in eight of his nine pro seasons. His career 5.2 yards-per-carry average is second all-time to Jamaal Charles of the Kansas City Chiefs (minimum 1,000 carries). Brown's 12,312 career rushing yards was a record that stood for 19 years and still ranks ninth all-time even though he retired at age 30.	**CAREER HIGHLIGHT**
1963 season: 1,863 rushing yards, 12 TDs, 6.4 yards per carry, 133.1 yards per game in 14 games	**BEST SEASON**
Brown was a star lacrosse player at Syracuse University. He is considered one of the greatest to ever play that sport.	**FUN FACT**
"He's just the best back in the league…fast as the fastest, hard as the hardest. He gets off to the quickest start of any big man I've ever seen. It's like tackling a locomotive." —Glenn Holtzman, defensive tackle, Los Angeles Rams, in 1958.	**QUOTABLE**

Backs

Adrian Peterson

2007–present

6'1", 217 pounds

Peterson is a strong runner who is a threat to break out on a long run on any given play. Simply put, he's like a modern day Jim Brown.

As a rookie in 2007, Peterson set the NFL single-game rushing record with 296 yards. In 2012, he had 2,097 rushing yards after coming back from a severe knee injury suffered during the final month of the 2011 season. He was named the 2012 NFL MVP.

2012 season: 2,097 rushing yards, 12 TDs, 6.0 yards per carry, 131.1 yards per game in 16 games

Peterson's dad gave him the nickname All Day as a kid because of Adrian's high energy level. He is still known as A.D.

"He has unbelievable vision, and not only does he see the first hole, but he also sees things on multiple levels. If you ask him what he saw, he would tell you he just felt it." —Toby Gerhart, running back, Minnesota Vikings, in 2013.

Running Backs

The ground game has been a huge part of football since the early days of the sport. Over the years, star rushers have developed signature playing styles, using their impressive skills in different ways to help their team move the ball. Here is a look at four kinds of running backs who have made a mark in the NFL.

~ 1980s ~
Bo Jackson

~ 1960s ~
Gale Sayers

BURNERS

Speed was the name of the game for these backs. Sayers busted out big gains as a running back and kick returner for the Chicago Bears. A star for the Los Angeles Raiders, Jackson ran the 40-yard dash in an estimated 4.12 seconds leading up to the 1986 draft. Johnson ran the 40 in 4.24 seconds at the 2008 draft combine, the best official time ever at the event. He had 2,006 rushing yards for the Tennessee Titans in 2009.

~ 2010s ~
Chris Johnson

LITTLE GUYS

Football may be a big man's game, but these diminutive players excelled on the gridiron. The 5'8" Sanders had a dizzying array of moves that helped him become one of the greatest backs of all time for the Detroit Lions. The 5'7" Jones-Drew combined speed and lower-body strength to reach double digits in TDs four times as a Jacksonville Jaguar. And the 5'6" Sproles emerged as one of QB Drew Brees's favorite targets for the New Orleans Saints.

~ 1990s ~
Barry Sanders

~ 2000s ~
Maurice Jones-Drew

~ 2010s ~
Darren Sproles

WORKHORSE

These guys carried the ball often, wearing down defenses with each touch. Campbell had at least 300 carries in a season five times for the Houston Oilers. Smith, who won three Super Bowls with the Dallas Cowboys, is the NFL's all-time leader in rushing yards (18,355) and carries (4,409). Lynch, a star for the Seattle Seahawks, totaled the most carries of any running back from 2011 through '13.

~ 1970s ~
Earl Campbell

~ 1990s ~
Emmitt Smith

~ 2010s ~
Marshawn Lynch

ALL-AROUND

Running backs weren't used much in the passing game until the mid-1980s, when the San Francisco 49ers' Roger Craig became the first to reach 1,000 receiving yards in a season, in 1985. Faulk was a superstar double threat for the St. Louis Rams — in 1999 he set the record for receiving yards by a running back (1,048). Tomlinson picked up where Faulk left off, becoming the second back to reach 100 receptions in a season, in 2003 for the San Diego Chargers. Today, McCoy of the Philadelphia Eagles is the most explosive dual-threat RB in the NFL. In 2013, he led the league in rushing and averaged 10.4 yards per reception, the highest of any running back.

~ 1990s ~
Marshall Faulk

~ 2000s ~
LaDainian Tomlinson

~ 2010s ~
LeSean McCoy

Tight Ends

A position once known for blocking has also turned out elite pass catchers

1960s

Mike Ditka
With 56 catches and 1,076 yards as a rookie for the Chicago Bears in 1961, Iron Mike changed how coaches viewed the tight end position. He later became the first tight end to be elected to the Pro Football Hall of Fame.

1970s

Charlie Sanders
Like many of the best pass-catching tight ends in the NFL today, Sanders was a basketball and football star in college. He led the Detroit Lions in receptions in six of his 10 NFL seasons.

1980s

Kellen Winslow Sr.
In his nine seasons with the San Diego Chargers, Winslow twice led the league in receptions. He had 89 catches in 1980 and 88 in '81.

Ozzie Newsome
Newsome was a driving force behind the Cleveland Browns' three AFC Championship Game appearances in the 1980s. He retired as the career leader among tight ends in catches and yards.

1990s

Shannon Sharpe
Known for his big-play ability for the Denver Broncos and Baltimore Ravens, Sharpe was the first tight end to reach 10,000 career receiving yards. He was inducted into the Hall of Fame in 2011.

2000s

Tony Gonzalez
A star for the Kansas City Chiefs and the Atlanta Falcons, Gonzalez had at least 90 receptions in a season five times, the most of any tight end. His 1,325 career catches are second all-time among all players and 446 more than the next-best tight end.

Antonio Gates
Gates showed just how well hardwood skills could translate to the gridiron. The former college hoops star had nine straight seasons with at least seven TDs for the San Diego Chargers even though he didn't play a down of NCAA football.

2010s

Jimmy Graham
Another ex-basketball player, Graham played one season of football at the University of Miami. He's now a top receiving threat for the New Orleans Saints, leading the NFL with 16 TD catches in 2013.

Total Control

Johnson's ability to shift his body in midair and position himself against defensive backs harkens back to **Lynn Swann**. The Pittsburgh Steelers Hall of Famer was the master of the circus catch, making tough grabs look routine in the 1970s.

Fancy Footwork

Every time Johnson fakes out a defensive back, you see a bit of **Don Hutson**. A member of the Green Bay Packers from 1935 through '45, Hutson had exceptional pass-catching and route-running skills, which inspired teams to embrace the air attack.

Wide Receivers

The most dominant pass-catcher of his generation, CALVIN JOHNSON of the Detroit Lions combines the skills of the greatest receivers of all time

Strong Man

Nicknamed Megatron, Johnson has strength that is unmatched at the receiver position. His power is reminiscent of **Tom Fears**, the Los Angeles Rams Hall of Famer from the 1940s and '50s. A former defensive player, Fears often outmuscled multiple defenders to catch tough passes in traffic, a skill that Johnson also boasts.

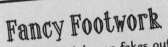

Short and Sweet

Johnson was once known for being primarily a downfield threat, but he has expanded his skills to become an elite possession receiver in the mold of the Denver Broncos' **Wes Welker**. In fact, 45 of Johnson's 84 receptions last season came on passes that traveled 10 yards or less, and he had an NFL-high 122 catches in 2012. Welker is the best possession receiver in today's game. He led the league in catches in 2007, '09, and '11.

Going Long

The 6'5", 239-pound Johnson is a big-time deep threat — he has scored 11 career touchdowns on passes thrown more than 30 yards. **Randy Moss**, at 6'4", 215 pounds, showed just how dominant a big wide receiver could be. He had 57 deep-ball TDs in 14 seasons (1998 through 2012).

1,964

Receiving yards accumulated by **Calvin Johnson** in 2012, an NFL single-season record. Johnson broke Jerry Rice's mark of 1,848, set in 1995, and averaged 122.8 yards a game that season.

Tireless Worker

Johnson is known for his strong work ethic, going all out even during practice, much like **Jerry Rice**, the greatest wide receiver in NFL history. A member of the San Francisco 49ers from 1985 through 2000, he was famous for his rigorous off-season routine, which included sprinting up hills.

The Defense

The Hall of Famers who set the gold standard on D and today's stars who follow in their footsteps

THEN

NOW

Safeties

Ronnie Lott

Lott started his career as a cornerback with the San Francisco 49ers but later moved to safety, where he made his mark. He had an uncanny ability to sense how a play was developing and would sprint over to deliver a crushing hit.

Troy Polamalu

With his long hair, Polamalu is easy to spot on the field — but tough to stop. Like Lott, he covers a lot of ground and makes tough tackles or interceptions. The four-time All-Pro helped the Pittsburgh Steelers win two Super Bowls.

Cornerbacks

THEN

NOW

Mel Blount

One of the best players of the 1970s, the 6'3", 205-pound Blount helped revolutionize the cornerback position by excelling in physical bump-and-run coverage on receivers. He was named the NFL's Defensive Player of the Year in 1975.

Richard Sherman

The Seattle Seahawks star is known for his trash talking, but he backs it up. A tall cornerback (6'3") in the mold of Blount, Sherman muscles up and shuts down superstar wideouts.

Defensive Ends

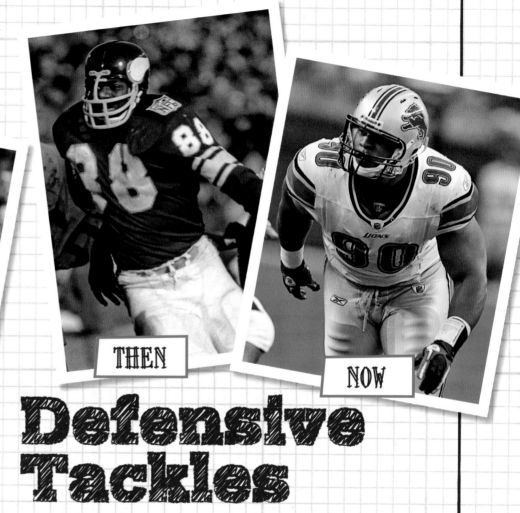

THEN

NOW

THEN

NOW

Defensive Tackles

Deacon Jones
THEN

A fearsome pass rusher in the 1960s and '70s, Jones coined the term *sack*. It was not an official stat during his playing days, but the eight-time Pro Bowler was estimated to have had multiple 20-sack seasons.

Jared Allen
NOW

Allen was the best pass rusher of the 2000s. The end recorded double-digit sacks in each of his six seasons with the Minnesota Vikings. He averaged 13 per year over his first 10 NFL seasons.

Alan Page

Page brought attention to a position that quietly does the dirty work. With a combination of size, strength, and speed, he was a looming presence on the dominant Vikings defenses of the 1970s. In '71, he became the first defensive player to win the NFL MVP.

Ndamukong Suh

Suh gained plenty of attention over his first four NFL seasons. A two-time first-team All-Pro with a nasty streak that opponents hate and teammates love, he has also put himself in the spotlight by starring in TV commercials.

Linebackers

⚬ 1950s ⚬
Chuck Bednarik

Even though he also played on offense, Bednarik made his mark at linebacker. The hard hitter became famous for his ferocious tackles, including a game-saving stop that clinched the 1960 title for the Philadelphia Eagles.

⚬ 1950s & '60s ⚬
Sam Huff

Huff defined the role of middle linebacker, becoming the leader of a talented New York Giants defense. He made a name for himself playing in New York — the five-time Pro Bowler even appeared on the cover of TIME magazine in 1959.

⚬ 1960s & '70s ⚬
Dick Butkus

They don't come any tougher than Butkus, an eight-time Pro Bowler for the Chicago Bears. Terrific at bringing down ball-carriers and picking off passes, he brought an intensity to the linebacker position that left a lasting impact.

⚬ 1970s ⚬
Jack Lambert

With his menacing toothless grin and imposing 6'4" build, Mad Man Jack was as intimidating as they come. He anchored Pittsburgh's Steel Curtain defense that won four Super Bowls in the 1970s.

They are playmakers, leaders, and bone-crushing tacklers. This position has set the tone for the NFL's greatest defenses

⚊ 1980s ⚊
Lawrence Taylor
The greatest linebacker of all time, L.T. was a master of taking down quarterbacks. He had double-digit sacks in seven seasons, and his 20½ sacks in 1986 are the most ever for a linebacker.

⚊ 1990s ⚊
Junior Seau
A respected leader and a polished all-round defender, Seau was selected to the Pro Bowl in 12 of his 20 seasons. He reached 100 tackles six times with the San Diego Chargers in the '90s.

⚊ 2000s ⚊
Ray Lewis
Lewis could cover the field like a free safety and make big plays by stuffing opposing running backs. Plus, the MVP of Super Bowl XXXV inspired teammates with his intense pregame speeches.

⚊ 2010s ⚊
Patrick Willis
Willis combines many of the skills of the classic linebackers before him. A tackling machine, he was selected to the Pro Bowl in each of his first seven seasons with the San Francisco 49ers.

kickers

The art of kicking has come a long way since the early days of the NFL

Making a field goal used to be tough. Like, *really* tough. Through the 1950s, kickers converted less than half of their attempts. But one man, Pete Gogolak, ushered in a new style that transformed the kicking game in 1964. Instead of running up to the ball from straight behind it, Gogolak used a soccer-style form, approaching his kicks from an angle. The swinging leg motion helped him get more velocity and better control. Gogolak was also one of the first players to specialize in kicking. Until then, most teams used linemen and other position players to boot field goals and extra points.

Other kickers soon adopted Gogolak's method, and field-goal percentages zoomed up. By the 1980s, kickers were making nearly 70 percent of their tries. In today's game, field goal kicking has become almost automatic. In 2013, 11 NFL kickers made more than 90 percent of their field-goal tries. Leading the way was Matt Prater of the Denver Broncos, who made 25 of 26 field-goal tries (96.2 percent), including an NFL-record 64-yarder on December 8, 2013.

Field-Goal Percentage for NFL Kickers

39.8
1940s

52.4
1960s

69.7
1980s

83.9
2010s

The Denver Broncos' Matt Prater booted a 64-yard field goal in Week 14 of the 2013 season, setting an NFL record.

Showmen

⇒ 1970s ⇐
Billy (White Shoes) Johnson

One of the originators of the end zone dance, the Houston Oilers receiver and returner would break into the Funky Chicken (followed by a split) after a TD.

⇒ 1980s ⇐
The Washington Redskins "Fun Bunch"

The Redskins made touchdown celebrations an organized team activity in the early '80s. After a score, the wide receivers and tight ends on the field would jump in the air for a group high five.

⇒ 1980s ⇐
Ickey Woods

The Cincinnati Bengals made a Super Bowl run in '88, and rookie running back Elbert (Ickey) Woods's 15 touchdowns were a big reason why. After a TD he would do the Ickey Shuffle, hopping on one leg, then the other, while switching the ball from hand to hand.

⇒ 1990s ⇐
Deion Sanders

Primetime showed that defensive players could be showmen too. The All-Pro cornerback was known for holding the ball in one hand and high-stepping his way to the end zone after interceptions.

With smooth moves and plenty of pizzazz, these players celebrated their touchdowns in style

⇒ 2000s ⇐
Terrell Owens

T.O. took end zone celebrations to another level in the early 2000s. He danced with a cheerleader's pom-poms, autographed the ball with a Sharpie that was hidden in his sock, and pretended to nap on the ball.

Terrell Owens 81

⇒ 2000s ⇐
Joe Horn

The New Orleans Saints wide receiver showed plenty of post-touchdown creativity. Horn's most bizarre celebration: hiding a cellphone in the padding of the goalpost and pretending to make a call after a TD.

⇒ 2010s ⇐
Victor Cruz

Largely due to Owens's and Horn's antics, the NFL began cracking down on excessive celebrations in the mid-2000s. But New York Giants wideout Cruz has kept the spirit alive by salsa dancing after TDs.

Records

These notable pro football single-season marks have gotten bigger over the years

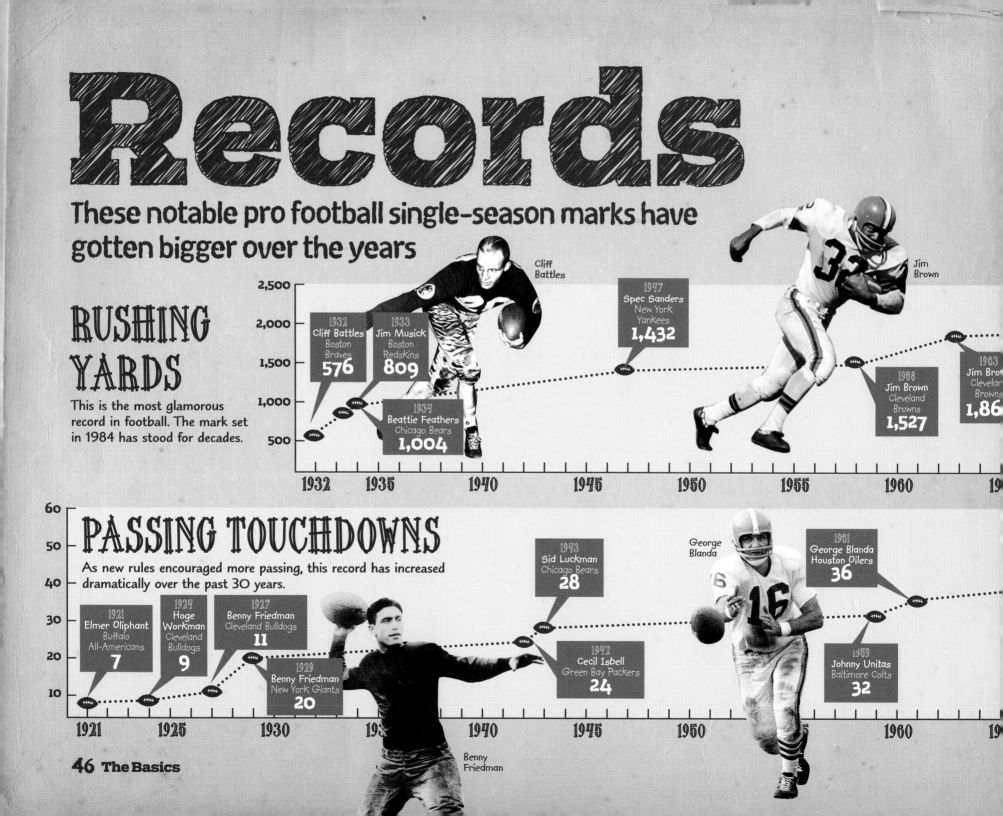

RUSHING YARDS

This is the most glamorous record in football. The mark set in 1984 has stood for decades.

Cliff Battles

Jim Brown

1932 Cliff Battles Boston Braves **576**

1933 Jim Musick Boston Redskins **809**

1934 Beattie Feathers Chicago Bears **1,004**

1947 Spec Sanders New York Yankees **1,432**

1958 Jim Brown Cleveland Browns **1,527**

1963 Jim Brown Cleveland Browns **1,86**

2,500
2,000
1,500
1,000
500

1932 1935 1940 1945 1950 1955 1960 19

PASSING TOUCHDOWNS

As new rules encouraged more passing, this record has increased dramatically over the past 30 years.

George Blanda

Benny Friedman

1921 Elmer Oliphant Buffalo All-Americans **7**

1924 Hoge Workman Cleveland Bulldogs **9**

1927 Benny Friedman Cleveland Bulldogs **11**

1929 Benny Friedman New York Giants **20**

1942 Cecil Isbell Green Bay Packers **24**

1943 Sid Luckman Chicago Bears **28**

1959 Johnny Unitas Baltimore Colts **32**

1961 George Blanda Houston Oilers **36**

60
50
40
30
20
10

1921 1925 1930 193 1940 1945 1950 5 1960 19

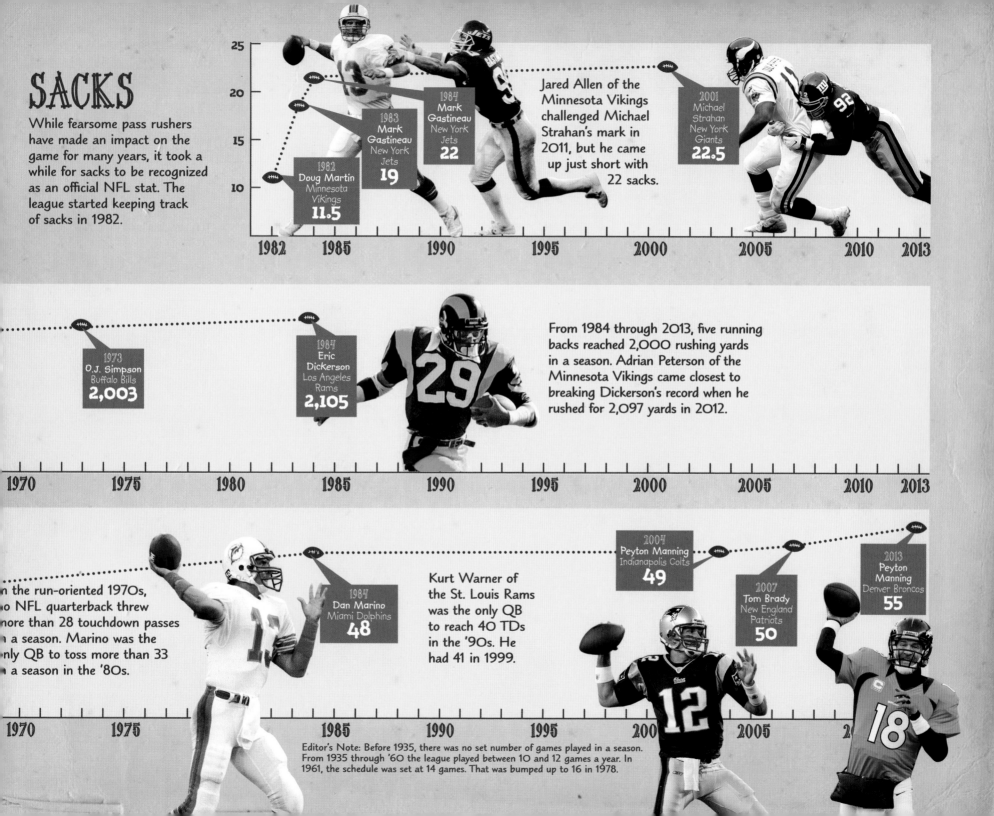

SACKS

While fearsome pass rushers have made an impact on the game for many years, it took a while for sacks to be recognized as an official NFL stat. The league started keeping track of sacks in 1982.

1982 Doug Martin Minnesota Vikings **11.5**

1983 Mark Gastineau New York Jets **19**

1984 Mark Gastineau New York Jets **22**

Jared Allen of the Minnesota Vikings challenged Michael Strahan's mark in 2011, but he came up just short with 22 sacks.

2001 Michael Strahan New York Giants **22.5**

1982   1985   1990   1995   2000   2005   2010   2013

1973 O.J. Simpson Buffalo Bills **2,003**

1984 Eric Dickerson Los Angeles Rams **2,105**

From 1984 through 2013, five running backs reached 2,000 rushing yards in a season. Adrian Peterson of the Minnesota Vikings came closest to breaking Dickerson's record when he rushed for 2,097 yards in 2012.

1970   1975   1980   1985   1990   1995   2000   2005   2010   2013

In the run-oriented 1970s, no NFL quarterback threw more than 28 touchdown passes in a season. Marino was the only QB to toss more than 33 in a season in the '80s.

1984 Dan Marino Miami Dolphins **48**

Kurt Warner of the St. Louis Rams was the only QB to reach 40 TDs in the '90s. He had 41 in 1999.

2004 Peyton Manning Indianapolis Colts **49**

2007 Tom Brady New England Patriots **50**

2013 Peyton Manning Denver Broncos **55**

1970   1975   1985   1990   1995   200   2005   2

Editor's Note: Before 1935, there was no set number of games played in a season. From 1935 through '60 the league played between 10 and 12 games a year. In 1961, the schedule was set at 14 games. That was bumped up to 16 in 1978.

In one sense, football is a very simple game: The goal is to get the ball into the end zone and score more points than your opponent. But moving the ball — and preventing the other team from doing so — has become a very complicated process. Today, pro football strategies feature a dizzying number of offensive and defensive schemes, creative ways of motivating and evaluating players, and the use of advanced technology.

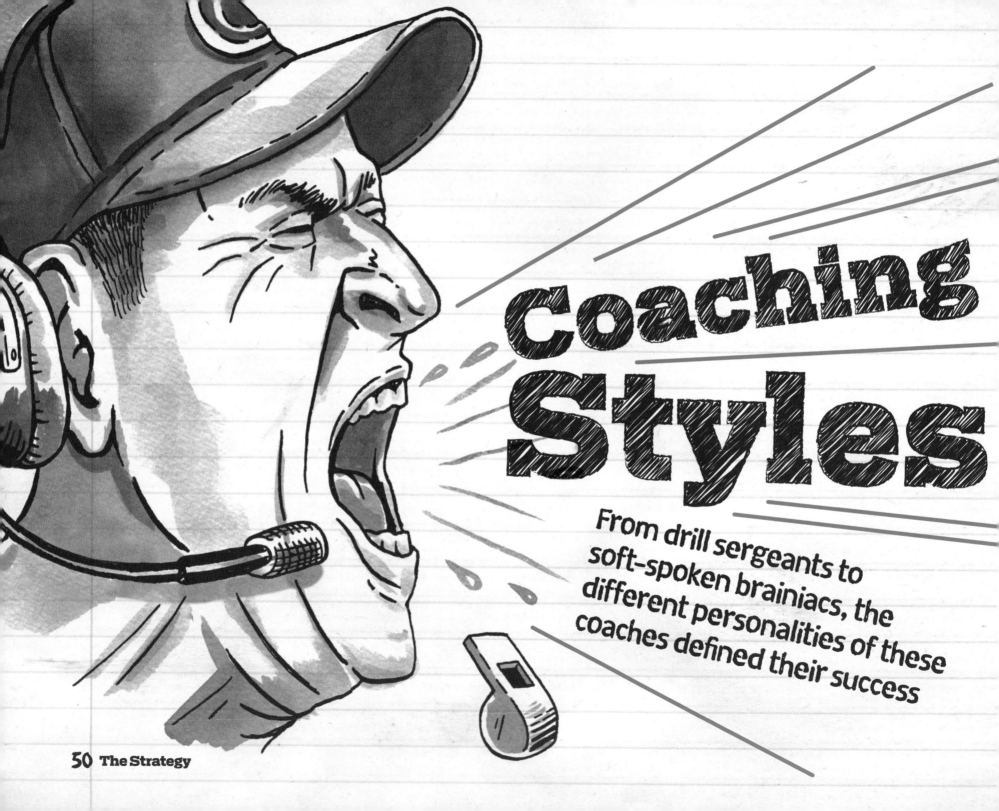

Coaching Styles

From drill sergeants to soft-spoken brainiacs, the different personalities of these coaches defined their success

MASTER MOTIVATORS

≠ 1960s ≠
Vince Lombardi
The legendary coach of the Green Bay Packers was known for his passionate speeches and for famous quotes like, "Winning isn't everything; it's the only thing."

≠ 1980s ≠
Joe Gibbs
Gibbs won the respect of his Washington Redskins teams with a cool demeanor and an unmatched ability to make key adjustments during pivotal moments.

≠ 2000s ≠
Mike Tomlin
With his confidence and poise, the Pittsburgh Steelers coach is a natural leader. In the 2008 season, he became the youngest head coach (age 36) to win a Super Bowl.

≠ 2010s ≠
Pete Carroll
A true players' coach, Carroll is known for pulling pranks during practice and creating a loose, fun atmosphere. His tactics worked — his Seattle Seahawks dominated the Denver Broncos to win Super Bowl XLVIII.

MASTERMINDS

≠ 1970s ≠
Tom Landry
As the defensive coordinator for the New York Giants in the 1950s, Landry invented the 4–3 defense. He later used the formation to win two Super Bowls as head coach of the Dallas Cowboys.

≠ 1970s ≠
John Madden
You may know him from his video game franchise, but the Oakland Raiders leader was also one of the smartest coaches of all time. He popularized studying game film to analyze opponents' strengths and weaknesses.

≠ 1980s ≠
Bill Walsh
The San Francisco 49ers coach is famous for designing the West Coast Offense, which calls for short, precise passes that allow the offense to keep possession of the ball longer.

≠ 2000s & '10s ≠
Bill Belichick
He first made a name for himself as a defensive genius. He later teamed with quarterback Tom Brady on the New England Patriots to orchestrate one of the highest-scoring offenses in NFL history.

TASKMASTERS

≠ 1950s ≠
Paul Brown
The Hall of Fame coach for the Cleveland Browns was the first to demand that his players sleep in a team hotel the night before home games in order to stay focused.

≠ 1980s & '90s ≠
Bill Parcells
Parcells held tough practices and was brutally honest when giving feedback to players. His style worked: He won two Super Bowls with the New York Giants.

≠ 2000s ≠
Tom Coughlin
The Giants coach was infamous for fining players if they didn't arrive at meetings five minutes early.

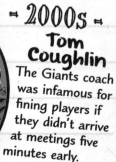

≠ 2010s ≠
Jim Harbaugh
Described as having a military style, the fiery Harbaugh won 36 games in his first three years leading the 49ers.

Offensive Systems

The development of formations from rushing to passing-based attacks

T-Formation

Considered the oldest formation in football, the T was said to have been invented by the father of the sport, Walter Camp, in the 1800s. With forward passing not yet allowed, this offense focused on the power rushing game. The quarterback would hand off to one of two halfbacks, who would then plow forward with the support of multiple blockers.

TE LT LG C RG RT TE

QB

HB FB HB

Single Wing

Coach Glenn (Pop) Warner is credited with inventing this offense in the early 1900s. Football teams were adjusting to the new rule that allowed forward passes, and Warner's Carlisle Indians had the greatest athlete of the time, the mighty Jim Thorpe. Playing the single wing tailback position, Thorpe was able to take the snap and run with the ball or throw downfield. Nearly a century later, a similar offense became popular in the NFL — it was called the Wildcat.

TE LG C RG RT RT TE

QB   WB

FB

TB

KEY: **QB** - Quarterback; **HB** - Halfback; **TB** - Tailback **FB** - Fullback; **WB** - Wingback; **TE** - Tight End; **LT** - Left Tackle; **LG** - Left Guard; **C** - Center; **RG** - Right Guard; **RT** - Right Tackle; **WR** - Wide Receiver

1960s to 1980s

Pro Set

This formation, with the QB under center, two backs split behind him, and two wide receivers, was the most common one in the second half of the 1900s. The West Coast offense, a pro-set offense that focuses on short passing routes, was made popular by Bill Walsh and the San Francisco 49ers in the 1980s, and is still used by teams today.

(WR) (LT) (LG) (C) (RG) (RT) (TE)

(QB) (WR)

(HB) (FB)

1970s to 2000s

Shotgun

Invented in the 1940s, this formation became popular thanks to QB Roger Staubach's successful use of it in the 1970s. In the shotgun, the quarterback takes the snap about five yards behind the line of scrimmage, which allows him to pass quickly without having to first take several steps in his dropback.

(WR) (LT) (LG) (C) (RG) (RT) (TE)

(WR) (WR)

(HB) (QB)

2010s

Pistol

This formation was designed in the mid-2000s for athletic quarterbacks who could run and pass. The QB takes the snap a few steps closer than the shotgun formation, giving the quarterback the advantage of a shotgun snap while allowing running plays to start closer to the line of scrimmage. This offense is tailor-made for a QB like Colin Kaepernick, who steered the 49ers deep in the playoffs in 2012 and '13.

(WR) (LT) (LG) (C) (RG) (RT) (TE)

(WR) (WR)

(QB)

(HB)

Defensive Systems

These schemes have shut down elite offenses over the years

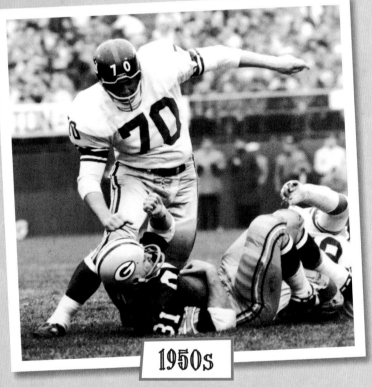

1950s

1960s & '70s

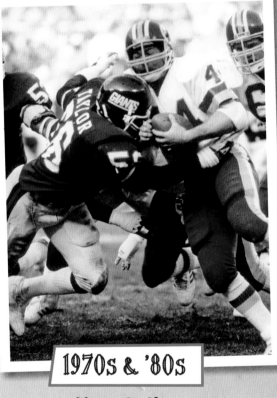

1970s & '80s

The 4-3

Tom Landry is credited with inventing this ground-breaking defense while serving as the New York Giants' defensive coordinator. The front seven consists of four down linemen and three linebackers. It was able to highlight the talents of Giants star linebacker Sam Huff *(above)*. Over the last decade, a majority of NFL teams have used a variation of the 4–3.

Nickel

The nickel uses five defensive backs to help control passing offenses. It was designed in the 1960s to contain Mike Ditka, the first tight end to be an effective pass catcher. In the '70s, Miami Dolphins coach Don Shula *(above, left)* used it with his dominant defense. Today, the nickel is used often to combat offensive schemes that involve extra receivers.

The 3-4

This defense became popular in the late 1970s. Using three down linemen and four linebackers, it is best suited for teams with terrific pass rushers in their linebacking corps. The New York Giants of the mid-'80s perfected this defense, with Hall of Fame linebacker Lawrence Taylor *(above)* putting heat on opposing offenses.

1980s

The 46

Designed by defensive coordinator Buddy Ryan, this defense made the Chicago Bears of the mid-80s arguably the greatest defense of all time. Ryan's philosophy was to put immense pressure on opposing QBs. He would rush the passer with six to eight defenders, forcing the opponent to make a quick (and often unwise) decision.

1990s

Miami 4-3 Front

Dallas Cowboys coach Jimmy Johnson *(above)* brought this style to the NFL from his stint at the University of Miami. It was a simplified version of the 4-3 defense that took advantage of smaller, well-rounded athletes that could attack from multiple positions. Johnson's approach worked with Dallas — he won three Super Bowls in the 1990s.

1990s & 2000s

Cover 2

A zone defense in which each safety is responsible for covering half the field, the Cover 2 proved to be effective in slowing down opponents' passing games. By the early 2000s, it was tweaked by Buccaneers coach Tony Dungy, whose Tampa 2 defense made use of versatile linebackers such as Derrick Brooks *(above)* who could play the role of a third deep-pass protector.

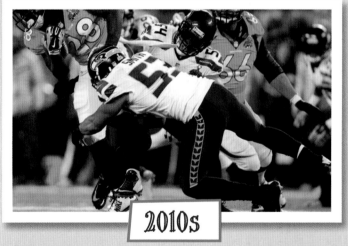

2010s

4-3 Scheme with 3-4 Personnel

Seattle Seahawks coach Pete Carroll has mixed two popular defenses to perfection. He has acquired big, physical linebackers that are a good fit for the 3-4 defense, but fast enough for a 4-3 scheme. The creativity has resulted in a lot of confusion for opposing offenses, and helped linebackers like Super Bowl XLVIII MVP Malcolm Smith *(above)* become tackling machines.

Championships

We analyzed every Super Bowl champion to find out whether the saying "Defense wins championships" is actually true

VINCE LOMBARDI
TROPHY

SUPER BOWL XXXVII
AFC vs NFC

1966	1971	1976	1981
Green Bay Packers	**Dallas Cowboys**	**Oakland Raiders**	**San Francisco 49ers**
OFF Rank: 15 DEF Rank: 3	OFF Rank: 1 DEF Rank: 3	OFF Rank: 2 DEF Rank: 18	OFF Rank: 13 DEF Rank: 2
Defense	Both	Offense	Defense
1967	1972	1977	1982
Green Bay Packers	**Miami Dolphins**	**Dallas Cowboys**	**Washington Redskins**
OFF Rank: 13 DEF Rank: 2	OFF Rank: 1 DEF Rank: 1	OFF Rank: 1 DEF Rank: 1	OFF Rank: 7 DEF Rank: 4
Defense	Both	Both	Defense
1968	1973	1978	1983
New York Jets	**Miami Dolphins**	**Pittsburgh Steelers**	**Los Angeles Raiders**
OFF Rank: 4 DEF Rank: 2	OFF Rank: 9 DEF Rank: 3	OFF Rank: 8 DEF Rank: 3	OFF Rank: 7 DEF Rank: 4
Both	Defense	Defense	Defense
1969	1974	1979	1984
Kansas City Chiefs	**Pittsburgh Steelers**	**Pittsburgh Steelers**	**San Francisco 49ers**
OFF Rank: 6 DEF Rank: 3	OFF Rank: 8 DEF Rank: 1	OFF Rank: 1 DEF Rank: 2	OFF Rank: 2 DEF Rank: 10
Defense	Defense	Both	Offense
1970	1975	1980	1985
Baltimore Colts	**Pittsburgh Steelers**	**Oakland Raiders**	**Chicago Bears**
OFF Rank: 8 DEF Rank: 9	OFF Rank: 7 DEF Rank: 4	OFF Rank: 16 DEF Rank: 11	OFF Rank: 7 DEF Rank: 1
Neither	Defense	Neither	Defense

Editor's Note: The offensive and defensive rankings are based on the regular season.

1986
New York Giants
OFF Rank: 10 DEF Rank: 2
Defense

1987
Washington Redskins
OFF Rank: 3 DEF Rank: 18
Offense

1988
San Francisco 49ers
OFF Rank: 2 DEF Rank: 3
Both

1989
San Francisco 49ers
OFF Rank: 1 DEF Rank: 4
Both

1990
New York Giants
OFF Rank: 17 DEF Rank: 2
Defense

1991
Washington Redskins
OFF Rank: 4 DEF Rank: 3
Both

1992
Dallas Cowboys
OFF Rank: 4 DEF Rank: 1
Both

1993
Dallas Cowboys
OFF Rank: 4 DEF Rank: 10
Offense

1994
San Francisco 49ers
OFF Rank: 2 DEF Rank: 8
Offense

1995
Dallas Cowboys
OFF Rank: 5 DEF Rank: 9
Offense

1996
Green Bay Packers
OFF Rank: 5 DEF Rank: 1
Both

1997
Denver Broncos
OFF Rank: 1 DEF Rank: 5
Both

1998
Denver Broncos
OFF Rank: 3 DEF Rank: 11
Offense

1999
St. Louis Rams
OFF Rank: 1 DEF Rank: 6
Offense

2000
Baltimore Ravens
OFF Rank: 17 DEF Rank: 2
Defense

2001
New England Patriots
OFF Rank: 19 DEF Rank: 24
Neither

2002
Tampa Bay Buccaneers
OFF Rank: 24 DEF Rank: 1
Defense

2003
New England Patriots
OFF Rank: 17 DEF Rank: 7
Neither

2004
New England Patriots
OFF Rank: 7 DEF Rank: 9
Neither

2005
Pittsburgh Steelers
OFF Rank: 15 DEF Rank: 4
Defense

2006
Indianapolis Colts
OFF Rank: 3 DEF Rank: 21
Offense

2007
New York Giants
OFF Rank: 16 DEF Rank: 7
Neither

2008
Pittsburgh Steelers
OFF Rank: 22 DEF Rank: 1
Defense

2009
New Orleans Saints
OFF Rank: 1 DEF Rank: 25
Offense

2010
Green Bay Packers
OFF Rank: 9 DEF Rank: 5
Defense

2011
New York Giants
OFF Rank: 8 DEF Rank: 27
Neither

2012
Baltimore Ravens
OFF Rank: 16 DEF Rank: 17
Neither

2013
Seattle Seahawks
OFF Rank: 18 DEF Rank: 1
Defense

Our Findings

Offensive-Oriented Teams **10 Times**	Defensive-Oriented Teams **19 Times**	Strong Offense and Defense **11 Times**

It's easy to see how strong defenses became associated with winning: Nine of the first 10 champions — including the first four — had defenses that ranked in the top 4 during the regular season. Of the 48 Super Bowl winners, 30 had top 5 defenses. Many of these powerhouse teams were strong on the other side of the ball as well — 21 squads had top 5 offenses. (The 1977 Cowboys were the only Super Bowl champs to lead the NFL in total offense *and* defense during the regular season.) Since 2000, six teams that weren't in the top 5 in defense or offense got hot in the postseason and won it all. Aside from these exceptions, is it generally true that defense wins championships? According to our analysis, the answer is yes.

Technology

How the NFL takes advantage of the Information Age

Today's NFL franchises rely on modern technology to stay on top. Thanks to computer programs and cutting-edge devices, teams can easily communicate with players, evaluate them, and get an entire offense and defense on the same page when executing complex strategies. The league has adapted new technologies to help improve the sport and protect the players. There's no doubt that the NFL is now wired to succeed.

Five Inventions That Are Changing the Game

Tablet Computers

Instead of lugging around hundreds of pages of printouts and stacks of DVDs, players now study playbooks and game film on portable tablets such as iPads. Tablet technology also has made it easier for coaches to update playbooks and send reminders to players about events like team meetings.

Instant Replay

First implemented in the 1986 season, instant replay has been huge in helping officials make sure they get the call right. The coaches' challenge system was introduced in 1999.

Coaches can disagree with a call, but risk losing a timeout if it is not overturned after being reviewed.

Advanced Statistical Analysis

Teams are hiring statisticians who look beyond basic numbers like yardage and total touchdowns. By using analytics and formulas, they create a wide range of reports for coaches and GMs, including ones that rate how a player's performance in college would translate to the NFL and when to go for it on fourth down.

Helmet Audio

Since 1994, NFL quarterbacks' helmets have had wireless audio capability so coaches can easily send plays and strategy to their signal-callers before the snap. Since 2008, two defensive players on each team have been allowed this feature in their helmets to communicate with defensive coaches.

Smart Mouthguards

Companies such as i1 Biometrics and X2 Biosystems have developed mouthguards that can gather data about the impact of a collision on a player's brain and send a report to a trainer or doctor on the sideline. This can potentially be a huge step in preventing and treating concussions.

1930s
Getting Started

The first NFL draft took place on February 8, 1936, at the Ritz-Carlton hotel in Philadelphia, Pennsylvania. Halfback Jay Berwanger, who was the first-ever Heisman Trophy winner, was the Number 1 pick that year, but he decided not to play pro football. He instead became a foam-rubber salesman, because it paid a higher salary. (The Philadelphia Eagles offered him between $125 and $150 per game, and later traded his rights to the Chicago Bears, who rejected his demand for $25,000 over two years.)

Making an Impact

The NFL upgraded to dry-erase boards by 1970. That year's draft was a notable one, as the Pittsburgh Steelers selected quarterback Terry Bradshaw with the first pick. Bradshaw would lead Pittsburgh to four Super Bowl titles during the decade.

1950s & '60s
Simple Times

Through the 1950s, the draft was not a huge event — and it had a whopping 30 rounds. In the '60s, it was still held in hotel ballrooms, with the commissioner writing teams' picks on a chalkboard.

1970s

The Draft

The biggest event of the modern NFL off-season — filled with wall-to-wall news coverage, predictions, and future stars — was once very low-key

DRAFT ON ESPN

RADE	TEAM	PLAYER	POSITION	GRADE
19.6		M. JUNKIN	ILB	18.9
9.5		R. BERNSTINE	TE	18.9
9.5		D. NOONAN	DT	18
9.4		N. ODOMES	CB	
9.2		P. PALMER	RB	
1		J. CLAY	OT	
1		H. BARTON	OT	18
1		K. FLOWERS	RB	
0		D.J. DOZIER	RB	
0	24	A. WHITE	S	
0		G. RAKOCZY	C	
0		K. STOUFFER	QB	
0	27	S. STEPHEN	OLB	
0		J. BOSA	DE	

1980s

Hitting the Airwaves

Just one year old at the time, ESPN started broadcasting the draft in 1980. By the late '80s, host Chris Berman helped transform the event into a made-for-TV affair.

1990s

In the Spotlight

Trimmed to eight rounds in 1993, the draft started to become the glamorous event we see today. The most notable pick of the '90s? None other than Peyton Manning, who was selected with the Number 1 pick of the '98 draft.

2000s & '10s

Prime Time

The draft was moved to Radio City Music Hall in 2006 and has become a highly anticipated red-carpet event. Fans fill the theater to see the top college players waiting for their names to be called by Commissioner Roger Goodell (pictured with Cam Newton in 2011). Teams also invite former stars to attend and participate. The draft is now a prime time show, surrounded by predictions and up-to-the-second updates from analysts and reporters.

The Scouting Combine

Evaluating talent has become close to a science

Finding elite talent has been a huge part of football since its early days. Teams have always had their eyes peeled for players who can help take their franchise to the top.

Scouting for talent is an art form. It takes a special eye to be able to evaluate players' abilities and decide whether they have what it takes to succeed on the game's highest level. The process has become streamlined thanks to the NFL Scouting Combine, which started in 1982. Each February, hundreds of prospects go to Indianapolis, Indiana, to take a set of medical, physical, and mental tests over a one-week span. The combine's profile has grown a lot over the years — it is now televised on the NFL Network, and the results are picked apart by scouts, general managers, media members, and fans alike.

While teams use the combine to help determine their draft strategy, it's not foolproof. In 1995, Boston College defensive end Mike Mamula was projected to be a third-round pick until an impressive performance at the combine propelled his draft stock. He was chosen seventh overall by the Philadelphia Eagles, but Mamula never lived up to the high pick — he had only 31.5 sacks over five NFL seasons. On the flip side, at the 2008 combine East Carolina running back Chris Johnson ran the 40-yard dash in 4.24 seconds, the fastest official time ever recorded at the event. He was chosen by the Tennessee Titans in the first round and won the rushing title in his second season, with 2,006 yards.

The combine has become particularly useful for finding diamonds in the rough. But in the end, the decision often comes down to grading players the old-fashioned way: how they've performed on the field during games.

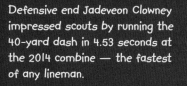

Defensive end Jadeveon Clowney impressed scouts by running the 40-yard dash in 4.53 seconds at the 2014 combine — the fastest of any lineman.

EXPERIENCE

What started as a game watched in person by a couple hundred people has blossomed into a multimedia extravaganza enjoyed by millions.

The Media

No longer just a radio broadcast, coverage of the NFL has exploded into an eye-popping multimedia bonanza

On October 22, 1939, NBC became the first TV network to broadcast a pro football game. Approximately 1,000 TV sets in New York showed the contest between the Brooklyn Dodgers and the Philadelphia Eagles.

1939

1934

The NFL's Thanksgiving Day game, on November 29, 1934 between the Chicago Bears and the Detroit Lions, was the first game to be broadcast nationally on the radio.

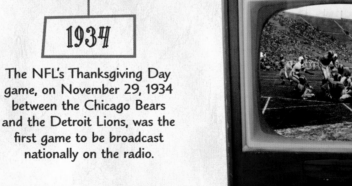

1970

As more people started purchasing TVs for their homes, the popularity of the NFL took off. Several star broadcasters emerged, including Howard Cosell, who did play-by-play for *Monday Night Football* from 1970 (its first season) through 1983. Cosell developed a signature style that included catchphrases such as, "He could go all the way!"

The 1981 season marked the beginning of the greatest partnership in football broadcasting history: John Madden *(right)* and Pat Summerall. The duo announced games with a mix of smarts and class. They worked together for 22 years.

1981

Print publications haven't just covered NFL news — they've also profiled the biggest stars and told great stories. Landing on the cover of *Sports Illustrated* — as Hall of Famers Joe Montana and Deion Sanders did in 1989 — is still a prestigious honor.

1989

1979

ESPN's Chris Berman *(below, left)* has played a big role in the development of media coverage of the NFL. An on-air personality since ESPN's first year (1979), he has anchored both *SportsCenter* and *Sunday NFL Countdown* since the 1980s. Berman's humorous and high-energy style have influenced many top announcers.

1986

Al Michaels *(right, with Cowboys QB Troy Aikman)* picked up *Monday Night Football* duties in 1986 and served as its play-by-play man for 20 years. Michaels had the longest tenure of any announcer in the program's history.

1990s

Fueled by the NFL's most exciting moments, highlight shows like *SportsCenter* thrived in the 1990s. The program is still at the top of its game with hosts such as David Lloyd *(above, left)* and Kevin Negandhi *(right)* at the helm.

The Internet helped expand coverage and brought fans closer to the game. By the mid-2000s, bloggers were able to join the conversation without needing a press pass. Platforms such as Twitter not only made sharing news easy and fast, it also allowed fans to connect directly with their favorite athletes and reporters. Longtime NFL writers such as Peter King *(left)* took their careers to another level with popular online columns.

Mid-2000s

Hoopla surrounding the sport reached a fever pitch in the 2000s. Glitzy pregame shows, such as the one produced by Fox Sports *(right)*, analyzed the matchups and the day's action before kickoff. ESPN's *Sunday NFL Countdown* expanded with features such as fantasy football tips. In 2003, the 24-hour NFL Network was launched.

Early 2000s

Sideline reporters have been a part of football telecasts since the 1970s, but these days many of them — such as Erin Andrews of Fox — have become as famous as the players.

2010s

SUPER BOWL XLVIII
NEW YORK · NEW JERSEY

4 RICHARD SHERMAN

2014

The coverage of the NFL has grown to serve a worldwide audience through many platforms — everything from radio to TV to laptop computers to cellphones. Just ask Richard Sherman of the Seattle Seahawks about how massive the coverage has gotten. The talkative cornerback was swarmed by hundreds of reporters at Super Bowl Media Day in 2014.

1972

Magnavox Odyssey

The Magnavox Odyssey was the first home video-game console. Football was one of the games that was included with it. The graphics were very basic. Players didn't even move their arms — they looked like tiny zombies!

1978

Atari Arcade

Video-game graphics hadn't improved much by the late 1970s, but there were more options for play calls. The emergence of arcade consoles made it possible for gamers to play each other head-to-head.

Tecmo Bowl

After success as an arcade game in 1987, *Tecmo Bowl* came to the Nintendo Entertainment System in '89. It featured figures that looked more human. *Tecmo Super Bowl*, released in '91, was groundbreaking for using the real names of NFL teams and players.

1987

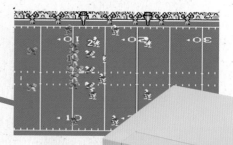

1988

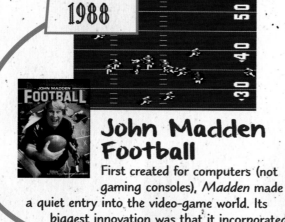

John Madden Football

First created for computers (not gaming consoles), *Madden* made a quiet entry into the video-game world. Its biggest innovation was that it incorporated weather conditions into games.

Madden NFL '94

By the mid-1990s, *Madden* started looking more like the game we know and love today. Real names of NFL teams were used, and full-season play was introduced.

1994

How football games went from dots on a screen to high-tech wonders

Video Games

1998

Madden NFL 2001

In 2000, EA Sports started putting NFL players on the cover of the game — Eddie George of the Tennessee Titans was the first to be featured. The PS2 and Xbox consoles resulted in even better graphics and allowed developers to add music soundtracks into the game.

2000

Madden NFL 99

Video game graphics took a big leap in the mid-'90s with the Sony PlayStation and Nintendo 64 platforms. The players in *Madden* started to look and move more realistically. Computer defenses in the game also became smarter, resulting in scores that were not as high as in the past.

Madden NFL 07

The next-gen consoles of PS3, Xbox 360, and Wii took gaming to a whole new level of realism and interactive capability. The player control — with an assortment of jukes and spins — became even more life-like. And, the ability to play online gave gamers the option to go head-to-head against competitors of all skill levels from anywhere in the world.

2006

2008

Madden NFL 09

Online leagues became fully developed, and the new Madden IQ tool allowed game play to be adjusted according to a player's skill level.

Madden NFL 25

The release of the Xbox One and PlayStation 4 made the graphics in *Madden* so detailed that it could be mistaken for a real NFL game on TV. The advancement of motion-capture technology fine-tuned players' signature moves and celebrations even more.

2013

The Super Bowl

How huge has the big game gotten? Ticket prices, the cost of TV commercials, and viewership have skyrocketed over the years.

1967

Most expensive ticket: $12

Price of 30-second commercial: $40,000

Number of people watching on TV: 24 million

1968

1976

1977

1978

1979

Average ticket price: $30

Price of 30-second TV commercial: $185,000

Number of people watching on TV: 75 million

1980

1981

1969

21 NA 76 99
Third World Championship Game

SUNDAY, JANUARY 12, 1969 • 3:00 PM
ORANGE BOWL, MIAMI, FLA. $12.00

1970

12 10 Z 17 or 18
SUPER BOWL
Fourth World Championship Game
Sunday, January 11, 1970 • 2:30 p.m.
Tulane Stadium, New Orleans,
ALL TAXES INCLUDED
$15.00

Fourth World Championship Game
Sunday, January 11, 1970 • 2:30 p.m.
Tulane Stadium, New Orleans,
NORTH END LOWER DECK $15.00
17 or 18 Z 10 12

1971

20 Z 75 81
SUPER BOWL V
AFC-NFC World Championship Game
Sunday, January 17, 1971 • 2:00 p.m.
Orange Bowl, Miami, Fla. • $15.00
All Taxes Included

1972

Z 68 50
SUPER BOWL VI
SUNDAY, JANUARY 16, 1972
KICKOFF 1:30 P.M. $15.00
AFC-NFC WORLD CHAMPIONSHIP GAME
SUNDAY, JANUARY 16, 1972 KICKOFF 1:30 P.M.
Tulane Stadium, New Orleans, Louisiana • $15.00

1973

50 90 51
SUPER BOWL VII
Sunday, January 14 1973
Kickoff 12:30 p.m. $15.00
all taxes included
AFC-NFC World Championship Game
SUNDAY, JANUARY 14, 1973 KICKOFF 12:30 P.M.
LOS ANGELES MEMORIAL COLISEUM • $15.00

1974

Lower West 109 42 97
STAND
SUPER BOWL VIII
Sunday, January 13, 1974
Kickoff 2:30 p.m. $15.00
all taxes included
AFC-NFC World Championship Game
Sunday, January 13, 1974
Rice Stadium, Houston, Texas $15.00

1975

Z 68 50
SUPER BOWL IX
Sunday, January 12, 1975
Kickoff 2:00 P.M. $20.00
all taxes included
AFC-NFC World Championship Game
Sunday, January 12, 1975 Kickoff 2:00 P.M.
Tulane Stadium, New Orleans, Louisiana • $20.00

1982

600 A 20
SUPER BOWL XVI
SUNDAY, JANUARY 24, 1982
KICKOFF 4:00 P.M. $40.00
All taxes included
NFC WORLD CHAMPIONSHIP GAME
Sunday, January 24, 1982 Kickoff 4:00 P.M.
Pontiac Silverdome $40.00

1983

H 100 80 40
SUPER BOWL XVII
ROSE BOWL
PASADENA
SUNDAY, JANUARY 30, 1983
KICKOFF 3:00 P.M. $40.00
GATES OPEN 12:15 P.M.
AFC-NFC WORLD CHAMPIONSHIP GAME
Sunday, January 30, 1983 Kickoff 3:00 P.M.
Rose Bowl, Pasadena, California • $40.00

1984

EAST 10 5
100 A 205
SUPER BOWL XVIII
SUNDAY, JANUARY 22, 1984
KICKOFF 4:30 P.M.
GATES OPEN AT 1:45 P.M.
$60.00 • ALL TAXES INCLUDED
AFC-NFC WORLD CHAMPIONSHIP GAME
SUNDAY, JANUARY 22, 1984 • KICKOFF 4:30 P.M.
TAMPA STADIUM, TAMPA, FLORIDA • $60.00

1985

6 55 10
4 12
GATE SECTION ROW SEAT
AFC-NFC WORLD CHAMPIONSHIP GAME
SUNDAY, JANUARY 20, 1985 KICKOFF 3:00 P.M.
STANFORD STADIUM $60.00

1986

K 386 06 20
LOGE
SUPER BOWL XX
AFC-NFC WORLD CHAMPIONSHIP GAME
Sunday, January 26, 1986
Louisiana Superdome $75.00
Sunday, January 26, 1986.
Kickoff 4:00 p.m. $75.00 All taxes included
GATE SECTION ROW SEAT
K 386 06 20
LOGE

1987

Z 30 90 45
GATE TUNNEL ROW SEAT
AFC-NFC World Championship Game
Sunday, January 25, 1987 3:00 PM
Rose Bowl, Pasadena, California $75.00
SUPER BOWL XXI
Sunday, January 25, 1987
3:00 PM Gates Open 12 Noon
$75.00 All Taxes Included
GATE TUNNEL ROW SEAT
Z 30 90 45

1988

T 70 10 10
GATE SECTION ROW SEAT
FIELD LEVEL
AFC-NFC World Championship Game
Sunday, January 31, 1988 3:00 p.m.
San Diego Jack Murphy Stadium $100.00
SUPER BOWL XXII
Sunday, January 31, 1988 Gates Open 12 Noon
San Diego Jack Murphy Stadium
$100.00 All Taxes Included
T 70 10 10
FIELD LEVEL

1989

LOWER

J	623	89	26
Gate	Section	Row	Seat

AFC-NFC WORLD CHAMPIONSHIP GAME
NFL
SUNDAY, JANUARY 22, 1989 • 5:00 PM
JOE ROBBIE STADIUM • MIAMI, FLORIDA $100.00

SuperBowl XXIII

SUNDAY, JANUARY 22, 1989 • GATES OPEN 3:00 PM
JOE ROBBIE STADIUM • MIAMI, FLORIDA
$100.00 ALL TAXES INCLUDED

Gate	Section	Row	Seat
J	623	89	26

LOWER

1990

TERRACE

X	724	12	15
GATE	SECTION	ROW	SEAT

NFL
AFC-NFC World Championship Game
Sunday, January 28, 1990 • 4:00 PM
Superdome • New Orleans $125.00

Sunday, January 28, 1990 • Gates Open 1:00 PM
Louisiana Superdome • New Orleans
$125.00 All Taxes Included

GATE	SECTION	ROW	SEAT
X	724	12	15

TERRACE

1991

EAST	3	66
STANDS	GATE	SEC.
65	27	27
AISLE	ROW	SEAT

NFL
SUNDAY, JANUARY 27, 1991
6:00 PM
GATES OPEN 3:00 PM
$150 ALL TAXES INCLUDED
AFC-NFC World Championship Game
Sunday, January 27, 1991 • 6:00 PM
TAMPA STADIUM, TAMPA, FLORIDA • $150

EAST	3	66
STANDS	GATE	SEC.
65	27	27
AISLE	ROW	SEAT

1992

I	192	01	26
GATE	SECTION	ROW	SEAT

AFC-NFC World Championship Game
Sunday, January 26, 1992 • 5:00 PM
Metrodome • Minneapolis, Minnesota
$150 All Taxes Included
Gates Open at 2:00 PM

SUPER BOWL XXVI

AFC-NFC World Championship Game
Sunday, January 26, 1992 • 5:00 PM
Metrodome • Minneapolis, Minnesota
$150 All Taxes Included

GATE	SECTION	ROW	SEAT
I	192	01	26

1993

V	87	83	80
GATE	TUNNEL	ROW	SEAT

NFL
AFC-NFC World Championship Game
Sunday, January 31, 1993 • 3:00 PM
Rose Bowl • Pasadena, California
$175 All Taxes Included
Gates Open at 12:00 PM

SUPER BOWL XXVII

AFC-NFC WORLD CHAMPIONSHIP GAME
SUNDAY, JANUARY 31, 1993 • 3:00 PM
ROSE BOWL • PASADENA, CALIFORNIA
$175 ALL TAXES INCLUDED

GATE	TUNNEL	ROW	SEAT
V	87	83	80

1994

1	01	30	94
GATE	SECTION	ROW	SEAT

LOWER LEVEL

AFC-NFC WORLD CHAMPIONSHIP GAME
SUNDAY, JANUARY 30, 1994 • 6:00 PM
GEORGIA DOME, ATLANTA
$175 ALL TAXES INCLUDED
Gates Open at 3:00 PM

SUPER BOWL XXVIII
NFL

AFC-NFC WORLD CHAMPIONSHIP GAME
SUNDAY, JANUARY 30, 1994 • 6:00 PM
GEORGIA DOME, ATLANTA
$175 ALL TAXES INCLUDED

LOWER LEVEL

GATE	SECTION	ROW	SEAT
1	01	30	94

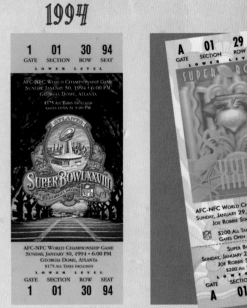

A	01	29
GATE	SECTION	ROW

LOWER LEVEL

SUPER BOWL

AFC-NFC WORLD CHAMP
SUNDAY, JANUARY 29, 19
JOE ROBBIE STADIUM
$200 ALL TAXES
GATES OPEN AT

Super Bowl
SUNDAY, JANUARY 29,
JOE ROBBIE STA
$200 ALL TAXE
LOW

GATE	SECTION	ROW
A	01	

2002

R	09	11	01
GATE	SECTION	ROW	SEAT

TERRACE

AFC-NFC WORLD CHAMPIONSHIP GAME
SUNDAY, FEBRUARY 3, 2002 • 5:00 P.M.
LOUISIANA SUPERDOME, NEW ORLEANS
$400 ALL TAXES INCLUDED
GATES OPEN AT 1:00 P.M.

SUPER BOWL XXXVI
SUNDAY, FEBRUARY 3, 2002 • 5:00 P.M.
LOUISIANA SUPERDOME, NEW ORLEANS
$400 ALL TAXES INCLUDED

TERRACE

GATE	SECTION	ROW	SEAT
R	09	11	01

2003

F	19	11	13
GATE	SECTION	ROW	SEAT

FIELD LEVEL

SUPER BOWL

AFC-NFC WORLD CHAMPIONSHIP GAME
SUNDAY, JANUARY 26, 2003, 3:00 P.M.
QUALCOMM STADIUM, SAN DIEGO
$400 ALL TAXES INCLUDED
GATES OPEN AT 11:00 A.M.

SUPER BOWL XXXVII
SUNDAY, JANUARY 26, 2003, 3:00 P.M.
QUALCOMM STADIUM, SAN DIEGO
$400 ALL TAXES INCLUDED
FIELD LEVEL

GATE	SECTION	ROW	SEAT
F	19	11	13

2004

A	138	A	15
GATE	SECTION	ROW	SEAT

LOWER LEVEL

SUPER BOWL XXXVIII

HOUSTON

AFC-NFC WORLD CHAMPIONSHIP GAME
SUNDAY, FEBRUARY 1, 2004 • 5:00 P.M.
Reliant Stadium, Houston
$500 EXEMPT FROM TEXAS STATE SALES TAX
GATES OPEN AT 1:00 P.M.

Super Bowl XXXVIII
SUNDAY, FEBRUARY 1, 2004 • 5:00 P.M.
Reliant Stadium, Houston
$500 (EXEMPT FROM TEXAS STATE SALES TAX)

LOWER LEVEL

GATE	SECTION	ROW	SEAT
A	138	A	15

2005

W	08	22	26
GATE	SECTION	ROW	SEAT

CLUB 39

SUPER BOWL XXXIX

JACKSONVILLE

AFC-NFC WORLD CHAMPIONSHIP GAME
SUNDAY, FEBRUARY 6, 2005 • 6:00 P.M.
ALLTEL STADIUM, JACKSONVILLE
$600 EXEMPT FROM FLORIDA
STATE SALES TAX
GATES OPEN AT 2:00 A.M.

SUPER BOWL XXXIX
SUNDAY, FEBRUARY 6, 2005 • 6:00 P.M.
ALLTEL STADIUM, JACKSONVILLE
CLUB 39

GATE	SECTION	ROW	SEAT
W	08	22	26

2006

08	22	26
SECTION	ROW	SEAT

CLUB/SUITE NORTH

SUPER BOWL XL

40TH ANNIVERSARY
ONE GAME, ONE DREAM
AFC-NFC WORLD CHAMPIONSHIP GAME
SUNDAY, FEBRUARY 5, 2006, 6:00 P.M.
FORD FIELD, DETROIT, MI
$700
GATES OPEN AT 2:00 P.M.

SUPER BOWL XL
SUNDAY, FEBRUARY 5, 2006, 6:00 P.M.
FORD FIELD, DETROIT, MI
CLUB/SUITE NORTH

SECTION	ROW	SEAT
08	22	26

2007

08	22	26
SECTION	ROW	SEAT

CLUB/SUITE

SUPER BOWL XLI

AFC-NFC WORLD CHAMPIONSHIP GAME
SUNDAY, FEBRUARY 4, 2007, 6:00 P.M.
DOLPHIN STADIUM, SOUTH FLORIDA
$700 GATES OPEN AT 2:00 P.M.
EXEMPT FROM FLORIDA STATE SALES TAX

SUPER BOWL XLI
SUNDAY, FEBRUARY 4, 2007, 6:00 P.M.
DOLPHIN STADIUM, SOUTH FLORIDA
CLUB/SUITE

SECTION	ROW	SEAT
08	22	26

2008

01	90	02
GATE	SECTION	ROW

MAIN LEVEL

SUPER BOWL XLII

AFC-NFC WORLD CHAMPIONSHIP
SUNDAY, FEBRUARY 3, 2008, 4
UNIVERSITY OF PHOENIX STADIUM
$700 GATES OPEN
AT 11:00 A.M.
ALL TAXES INCLUDED

SUPER BOWL XLII
SUNDAY, FEBRUARY 3, 2008, 4
UNIVERSITY OF PHOENIX STADIUM
MAIN LEVEL

GATE	SECTION	ROW
01	90	02

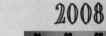

ge ticket price:

$200

Price of
-second TV
ommercial:

**$1
million**

ber of people
ching on TV:

**94
million**

Average ticket
price:
$3,715

Price of 30-second
TV commercial:

**$4
million**

Number of people
watching on TV:

**112
million**

Points Allowed
Passing TD 4 PTS
FUMBLES LOST = -2
TEs
Rushing Yards
TD = 6 PTS
*

.5 PTS/Reception
RUSHING TD 6 PTS

FANTASY STATS

XPT = 1
Sleeper Picks *
QBs
1PT/10 Rushing Yards
Flex Position
%

PLAYER RANKING

Fantasy Football

As technology has advanced, so has the game that gives fans a chance to be in charge of a team

It all started in 1960, when Bill Winkenbach, a part-owner of the Oakland Raiders, invented a game to play with his football-obsessed buddies. Eight guys would draft a roster of 20 NFL players, and they would score points corresponding to how those players performed in real games. The Greater Oakland Professional Pigskin Prognosticators League, as it was called, is considered the first-ever fantasy football game.

Fast-forward more than 50 years, and fantasy football has become a phenomenon on a mass scale. It is a computerized game played by millions of fans that generates billions of dollars. More so than fantasy games in other sports, the NFL's one-game-per-week schedule has proven to be ideal for people who want to invest a lot of time and effort into their team, or simply play casually as a way to enhance their NFL-watching experience and bond with friends.

The rise of fantasy football has mirrored the

development of advanced computers and high-speed Internet in the Information Age. The game started to pick up steam in 1993 with the release of the Fantasy Football League Manager (FFLM) program for personal computers. FFLM compiled stats and points so the owners could focus on the fun stuff: managing their rosters and trash-talking with their opponents. The FFLM program had about 20 customers in its first year. By 1999, it was used by 7,000 leagues.

That was nothing compared to what was coming in the years ahead. The late 1990s saw the rapid development of the Internet, and by the early 2000s fantasy football was offered on many major sports websites. This was huge, as fans could now easily sign up and play with user-friendly drafting and waiver-wire tools, and see real-time stats and player updates. Features were enhanced throughout the 2000s — special TV packages and online streaming video allowed fans to watch their fantasy players from anywhere. Mobile-phone apps showed scores in real time. And 'round-the-clock coverage of fantasy news dominated the airwaves.

By 2013, nearly 26 million people were playing fantasy football in the U.S. It's easy to see that the game has come a long way since 1960. However, one thing has remained the same: It has provided the perfect way for fans to feel the excitement of managing a team of stars and leading it to glory.

Fantasy Football Hall of Fame

Marshall Faulk

Faulk was a dual threat who piled up yards (and points for his fantasy owners) on the ground and in the air. In 2000, he had 1,359 rushing yards, 830 receiving yards, and 26 total TDs.

LaDainian Tomlinson

For most of the 2000s, fantasy owners with the top pick in their draft had an easy decision: Take L.T. Tomlinson's best season came in 2006, when he scored an NFL-record 28 rushing TDs.

Shaun Alexander

Touchdowns are huge in fantasy football, and Alexander racked them up in the 2000s. The Seattle Seahawks running back had five straight seasons with at least 16, including a then-NFL-record 28 total TDs in '05.

Randy Moss

No receiver carried a fantasy team like Moss. He had eight seasons with at least 10 receiving TDs, and his epic 2007 season (98 receptions, 1,493 yards, 23 TDs) helped many owners to a league title.

Peyton Manning

QBs are sometimes overlooked in fantasy football. Manning's performances in 2004 (49 passing TDs) and 2013 (55 TDs) made owners who chose a running back in Round 1 regret their decision.

The Fan

Back in the 1940s and '50s, fans were dapper ladies and gents. Today, rooting for a team means immersing yourself in the game in every way imaginable. And we mean *every* way.

THEN

NOW

PHOTO CREDITS

FRONT COVER AP (Baugh); Tony Tomsic/WireImage.com (Graham); Tony Tomsic/Getty Images (Unitas); Heinz Kluetmeier/Sports Illustrated (Bradshaw); John Iacono/Sports Illustrated (Montana); Simon Bruty/Sports Illustrated (Manning); Robert Beck/Sports Illustrated (Wilson)

TITLE PAGE Kidwiler Collection/Diamond Images/Getty Images (Unitas); John W. McDonough/Sports Illustrated (Manning); Courtesy Pro Football Hall of Fame (footballs)

THE BALL (PAGES 10–11) Courtesy Pro Football Hall of Fame (8); Bruce Bennett Studios/Getty Images (Mara)

SHOULDER PADS (PAGES 12–13) Courtesy of Pro Football Hall of Fame (1800s, 1920s, 1940s, 1960s, 1980s); David Berkwitz for Sports Illustrated (1930s); Bill Frakes/Sports Illustrated (2010s)

HELMETS (PAGES 14–15) Courtesy Pro Football Hall of Fame (6); NFL/WireImage.com (1980s); Bill Frakes/Sports Illustrated (2010s)

STADIUMS (PAGES 16–19) Pro Football Hall of Fame/WireImage.com (1932 game); Greg Nelson for Sports Illustrated (Cowboys stadium); Kirby Lee/US PRESSWIRE (general view of University of Phoenix Stadium); Gene Lower/Getty Images (University of Phoenix Stadium with roof open)

SALARIES (PAGES 20–21) Courtesy of Yale Athletics (Heffelfinger); Bettman Corbis (Thorpe); Neil Leifer/Sports Illustrated (Brown); Mark A. Wallenfang/WireImage.com (Favre); Robert Beck/Sports Illustraed (Rodgers); Getty Images (money)

STATS (PAGES 22–23) Heinz Kluetmeier/Sports Illustrated (Rodgers) Carlos M. Saavedra for Sports Illustrated (Peterson); George Bridges/MCT/Getty Images (Watt); Leon Halip/Getty Images (Johnson); Chris Szagola/CSM/Landov (Thomas); Jerome Davis/Icon SMI (Revis)

QUARTERBACKS (PAGES 28–29) Bettmann/Corbis (Baugh); Vic Stein/NFL Photos/AP (Graham); Yale Joel//Time Life Pictures/Getty Images (Unitas); Focus on Sport/Getty Images (Bradshaw); George Rose/Getty Images (Montana) Peter Read Miller for Sports Illustrated (Elway); Bob Rosato/Sports Illustrated (Manning, 2); Robert Beck/Sports Illustrated (Wilson); Diamond Images/Getty Images (Namath); Simon Bruty/Sports Illustrated (Vick); John Biever/Sports Illustrated (Brady); Peter Read Miller for Sports Illustrated (Elway arm); Hy Peskin/Sports Illustrated (Graham legs)

RUNNING BACKS (PAGES 30–33) Walter Iooss Jr. for Sports Illustrated (Brown, Sayers); Al Tielemans/Sports Illustrated (Peterson, McCoy); Richard Mackson for Sports Illustrated (Jackson); Bob Rosato/Sports Illustrated (Johnson); John Iacono/Sports Illustrated (Campbell); Tom Dipace (Smith); Steve Dykes/Getty Images (Lynch); Scott Halleran/Getty Images (Sanders); Sam Greenwood/Getty Images (Jones-Drew); Chris Graythen/Getty Images (Sproles); Peter Read Miller/Sports Illustrated (Faulk); John W. McDonough/Sports Illustrated (Tomlinson)

TIGHT ENDS (PAGES 34–35) NFL/WireImage.com (Ditka); Rich Clarkson/Rich Clarkson Associates/AP (Sanders); Heinz Kluetmeier/Sports Illustrated (Winslow); Focus on Sport/Getty Images (Newsome); Brian Bahr/Getty Images (Sharpe); Larry French/Getty Images (Gonzalez); Donald Miralle/Getty Images (Gates); Bill Frakes/Sports Illustrated (Graham)

WIDE RECEIVERS (PAGES 36–37) Jose Juarez/AP (Johnson); Walter Iooss Jr./Sports Illustrated (Swann); International News Photos (Hutson); Vic Stein/Getty Images (Fears); Scott Cunningham/Getty Images (Welker); John W. McDonough/Sports Illustrated (Moss); Peter Read Miller for Sports Illustrated (Rice)

THE DEFENSE (PAGES 38–39) Stephen Dunn/Getty Images (Lott); Peter Read Miller/Sports Illustrated (Polamalu); NFL Photos/AP (Blount); John W. McDonough/Sports Illustrated (Sherman); Tony Tomsic for Sports Illustrated (Jones); John Biever/Sports Illustrated (Allen); Focus on Sport/Getty Images (Page); Peter Read Miller/Sports Illustrated (Suh)

LINEBACKERS (PAGES 40–41) Robert Riger/Getty Images (Bednarik); Neil Leifer/Sports Illustrated (Butkus); Heinz Kluetmeier for Sports Illustrated (Lambert); Andy Hayt for Sports Illustrated (Taylor); Matt Brown/Newsport (Seau); Larry French/Getty Images (Lewis); Jed Jacobsohn for Sports Illustrated (Willis)

KICKERS (PAGES 42–43) Justin Edmonds/Getty Images (Prater)

SHOWMEN (PAGES 44–45) Houston Chronicle/AP (Johnson); Walter Iooss Jr. for Sports Illustrated (Redskins); Peter Read Miller for Sports Illustrated (Woods); Kevin Terrell/ WireImage.com (Sanders); Andy Hayt/Sports Illustrated (Owens); Chris Graythen/Getty Images (Horn); Rich Kane/Icon SMI (Cruz)

RECORDS (PAGES 44–45) Ronald C. Modra/Sports Imagery/Getty Images (Gastineau, Marino); Jim Turner/WireImage.com (Strahan); Pro Football Hall Of Fame/WireImage.com (Battles); Neil Leifer /Sports Illustrated (Brown); Michael Yada/Getty Images (Dickerson); Bettmann/Corbis (Friedman); Hy Peskin for Sports Illustrated (Blanda); Damian Strohmeyer/Sports Illustrated (Brady); John Biever/Sports Illustrated (Manning)

COACHING STYLES (PAGES 50–51) Neil Leifer/Sports Illustrated (Lombardi); Ron Heffin/AP (Landry); Neil Leifer/Sports Illustrated (Brown); Heinz Kluetmeier/Sports Illustrated (Gibbs); Mickey Pfleger for Sports Illustrated (Walsh); Ronald C Modra/Sports Imagery/Getty Images (Parcells); Jason Bridges/Us Presswire (Tomlin); James Drake for Sports Illustrated (Madden); Al Tielemans/Sports Illustrated (Coughlin); Otto Greule Jr/Getty Images (Carroll);

Damian Strohmeyer/Sports Illustrated (Belichick); Chris Graythen/Getty Images (Harbaugh)

OFFENSIVE SYSTEMS (PAGES 52–53) Bettmann/Corbis (Thorpe); Pro Football Hall Of Fame/WireImage.com (Bears); George Long/LPI/WireImage.com (Montana); Lane Stewart/Sports Illustrated (Staubach); Robert Beck/Sports Illustrated (Kaepernick)

DEFENSIVE SYSTEMS (PAGES 54–55) Robert Riger/Getty Images (Huff); Focus on Sport/Getty Images (Shula); Focus on Sport/Getty Images (Taylor); John Iacono/Sports Illustrated (Dent); George Rose/Getty Images (Johnson); Craig Lassig/AFP (Brooks); Bill Frakes/Sports Illustrated (Smith)

CHAMPIONSHIPS (PAGES 56–57) David E. Klutho/Sports Illustrated (Trophy)

TECHNOLOGY (PAGES 58–59) Wesley Hitt/Getty Images (helmet headset); Patrick McDermott/Getty Images (replay booth); Courtesy X2 Impact (mouthguard); Sam Greenwood/Getty Images (coach)

NFL DRAFT (PAGES 60–61) NFL Photos/AP (1965 draft); HH/AP (Rozelle); Paul Spinelli/AP (Berman); Adam Nadel/AP (Manning); David Bergman for Sports Illustrated (Goodell with Newton)

THE COMBINE (PAGES 62–63) Joe Robbins/Getty Images (Clowney)

MEDIA (PAGES 66–69) Getty Images (radio); Douglas Davidian/iStockphoto/Getty Images (1940s TV); Focus on Sport/Getty Images (Cosell); Wally McNamee/Bettman Corbis (Summerall and Madden); Lee Crum for Sports Illustrated (Sanders on Sports Illustrated); John Iacono/Sports Illustrated (Montana on Sports Illustrated); Rick LaBranche/ESPN Images (Berman); James D. Smith/WireImage.com (Michaels); Todd Rosenberg for Sports Illustrated (King); Mark Cunningham/Detroit Lions/Getty Images (Fox Sports); Paul Sancya/AP (Andrews); Jeff Zelevansky/Getty Images (Sherman); Todd Cordoza/Getty Images (TV)

VIDEO GAMES (PAGES 70–71) Courtesy Magnavox (Magnavox Odessey); Courtesy Atari Inc. (Atari console); Courtesy Nintendo (Nintendo 1987, Wii); Courtesy Sony Computer Entertainment America (PS2, PS4); Courtesy Microsoft (Xbox); Courtesy EA Sports (Madden images, 14)

SUPER BOWL (PAGES 72–75) Courtesy NFL (48)

FANTASY (PAGES 72–75) Gary Brady/Reuters (Faulk); Simon Bruty/Sports Illustrated (Tomlinson); Peter Read Miller/Sports Illustrated (Alexander); Jim Rogash/Getty Images (Moss); Andrew Hancock for Sports Illustrated (Manning)

BACK COVER Courtesy Pro Football Hall of Fame (6); NFL/WireImage.com (Cowboys); Michael J. LeBrecht II for Sports Illustrated (Packers)

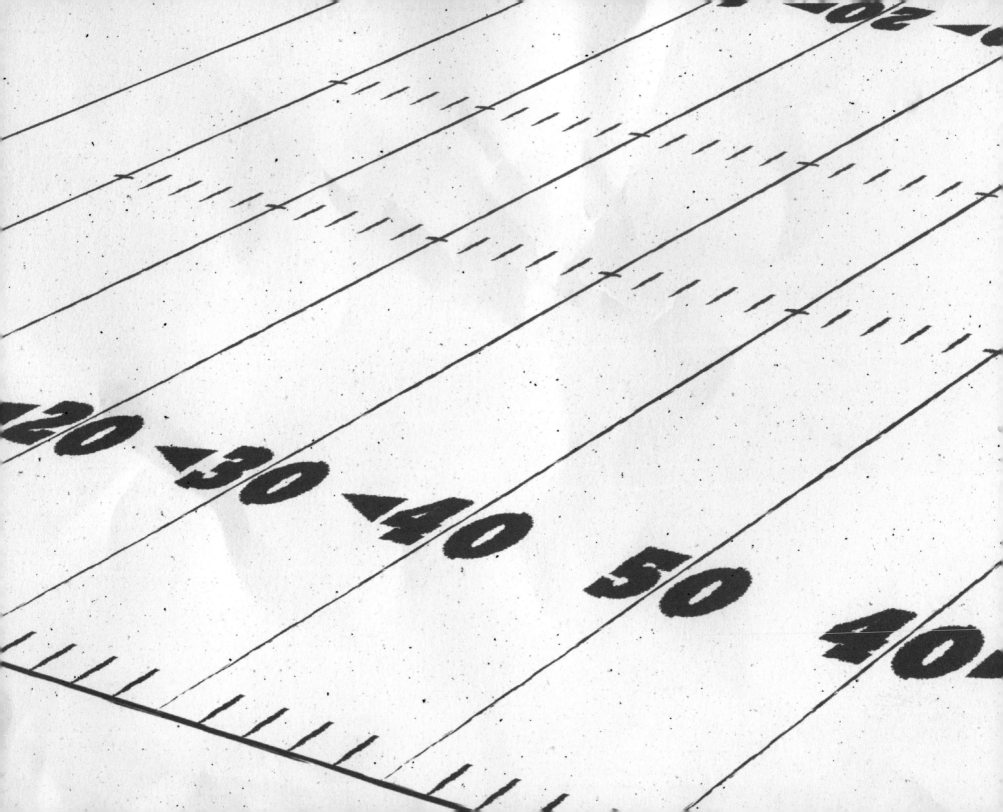